Logistics *and* Transportation

Linda Stanley, Ph.D. *and*
Darin Matthews, CPPO, C.P.M.

Prepared for NIGP: The Institute for Public Procurement. All rights are conveyed to the NIGP upon completion of this book.

Logistics and Transportation

Information in this book is accurate as of the time of publication and consistent with generally accepted public purchasing principles. However, as research and practice advance, standards may change. For this reason, it is recommended that readers evaluate the applicability of any recommendation in light of particular situations and changing standards.

National Institute of Governmental Purchasing, Inc. (NIGP)
151 Spring Street
Herndon, VA 20170
Phone: 703-736-8900; 800-367-6447
Fax: 703-736-9639 Email: education@nigp.org

This book is available at a special discount when ordered in bulk quantities. For information, contact NIGP at 800-367-6447. A complete catalog of titles is available on the NIGP website at www.nigp.org.

ISBN 1-932315-10-1
ISBN 978-1-932315-10-3

This book was set in Berkeley Oldstyle
Design & production by Vizual, Inc. - www.vizual.com.
Printed & bound by HBP.

Acknowledgements

This book has been a rewarding journey. From the first text-writing symposium, co-sponsored by NIGP and Florida Atlantic University, it has been a privilege working with colleagues in public procurement as well as the academic community. From the beginning, LEAP combined the best of both worlds.

I was fortunate in getting paired with Dr. Linda Stanley, an expert in the field of supply management and logistics. Her patience and professionalism are unparalleled.

Many dear friends and associates have contributed to *Logistics and Transportation*, far too many to mention. Thank you all for the forthright review and feedback. This book would not have been possible without the knowledge and experience within the NIGP instructor ranks and our professional staff at NIGP headquarters.

I would also like to thank my father, James Quincy Matthews, who taught me the importance of integrity, whether you're building cabinets or contracts.

Darin L. Matthews, CPPO, C.P.M.

My heartfelt thanks go out to the people at NIGP and Florida Atlantic University who brought me into this writing project.

I also thank Darin Matthews, my writing partner, who shared his many years of public procurement experience and made the writing process a smooth one.

Many others in the field of public procurement shared their wisdom, provided invaluable feedback throughout the project, and made the book what it is. The finished product would also not have been possible without the help of the professional staff at NIGP.

Lastly, I would like to thank my husband Kim for supporting with me throughout the writing process. His ability to make me laugh during the stressful times has been a true blessing.

Linda Stanley, Ph.D.

Contents

Chapter 1

Logistics and Transportation - Overview

The management of transportation services is frequently an overlooked opportunity to contribute to the success of governmental and not-for-profit operations that depend on purchasing's ability to evaluate and make transportation decisions. Many public purchasers are not familiar with the costs of transportation and unaware of potential opportunities for savings. Traditionally, the procurement and management of transportation services has been relegated to the supplier who provides a "laid down price" or "landed cost"—the cost of transportation rolled into the price of purchased goods. The advantage of this situation lies in the competitive bidding process, where a buyer can easily compare quotes to determine the lowest landed cost. In many instances, this is the only option given to the public purchaser. This type of operation was particularly popular in the late 1970s because rates were regulated by federal and state governments and not negotiable.

There are a number of reasons public purchasers should have a better understanding of the transportation decision. First, there is a cost attached to delegate the decision to the supplier. For example, suppliers often add a fixed amount for transportation based on the purchase price, which is higher than the actual amount charged by the transportation provider. Without a clear understanding of the transportation industry, the purchasing officer trusts the supplier to charge fairly for this service. The supplier should, at a minimum, disclose transportation charges. The next step is negotiating directly with a few transportation providers and consolidating shipments, resulting in significant cost savings. Secondly, consolidation and control translates into strength with the transportation provider, resulting in better service. Specific needs, such as special drop-off points, deliveries during certain operating hours, or shipments on specific pallet sizes, are now possible. If left to the supplier, service needs may not be met. Often, carriers are operating as logistics service companies and will integrate their expertise with that of their customers (Stock, 1988). Finally, as public purchasing moves toward more contract negotiation, understanding the transportation portion of the contract is critical. Government agencies have begun to realize the value of evaluating the *total cost* of procuring goods, which may include transportation costs, carrying costs or disposal costs, among other things. Consideration of these costs is more involved in contract negotiations today.

Thus, savings opportunities and more service options are possible by paying closer attention to the details of the transportation decision, whether directly arranged by the procurement officer or managed by a supplier. Components of the transportation service purchasing function include (a) evaluating the prices of various transportation methods; (b) determining the effect of transportation service on operations; and (c) evaluating the effect of transit times, carrier dependability, and safe delivery on inventory levels (National Institute of Governmental Purchasing, Inc. [NIGP], 2000). Other important decisions include (a) the selection of options and carriers; (b) reduction of transportation and inventory carrying costs; (c) expediting and tracing shipments; and (d) processing claims. The selection of a transportation system is a specialized form of procurement in which services are purchased to provide a link among manufacturing sites, warehouses, distribution centers, and/or office sites.

Common Transportation/Logistics Terms

Transportation is "the physical movement of goods and people between points" (Wood & Johnson, 1995, p. 4). Purchased goods may include new materials brought into a production process or finished goods shipped to the customer. A *consignee* is the party, usually the buyer, who receives the goods sent by the *consignor*, usually the seller.

Carriers are those organizations that provide transportation services, and primary *modes* include railroads, motor carriers, airlines, water carriers, and pipelines. The supplier or the buying organization may do contracting for transportation and related services. The party responsible for arranging transportation is the *shipper*.

Shippers may also hire *third party logistics providers* (3PLs), or intermediaries, who serve to coordinate the various modes of transportation for shipment from supplier to buyer, and may offer other services. Some examples of 3PLs include *transportation brokers*, *freight forwarders*, and *shippers' associations*. *Transportation brokers* locate carriers for shippers, consolidate shipments, and charge a certain percentage of the rate to the shipper. *Freight forwarders* help in the movement of shipments by combining less than carload (LCL) or less-than-truckload (LTL) into carload (CL) or truckload (TL) lots. The freight forwarder pays the transportation carrier on the basis of CL or TL rates but charges the shipper on LCL or LTL rates, which are higher. *Shippers' associations* are not-for-profit organizations acting as freight forwarders. Any profits obtained through consolidation of shipments are returned to the shippers.

Transportation is an integral part of both the inbound and outbound movements of goods. The inbound side is often referred to as *materials management*, which combines the activities of procurement, warehousing, transportation, inventory management, quality control, and scrap/disposal with the goal of improved customer service (Coyle, Bardi, & Langley, 1996; Heizer & Render, 2001). *Physical distribution* focuses on the outbound side, dealing with the flow of finished goods to the final customer (Coyle et al., 1996). There may be several channel members in the physical distribution of goods, including wholesalers and distributors. *Logistics management* or *integrated logistics management* combines both the inbound and outbound sides and can be defined as "the art and science of obtaining and distributing materials and products" (NIGP, p. 47).

Evolution of Logistics

The term *logistics* was derived from military activities related to deployment and support of armed forces during times of war (Gourdin, 2001). In fact, logistics was referred to as early as 500 BC in *The Art of War* (Tzu & Gagliardi, 1999), a book about logistical activities and their relationship to war tactics and strategies. During World War II, logistical activities contributed to victory for the United States and its allies. Since the 1960s, logistics has moved to the forefront of best business practices. More recently, logistical activities were identified as a critical component of success for the United States during the Gulf War in 1990-1991. A massive movement of 122 million meals, 1.3 billion gallons of fuel, and 31,800 tons of mail was involved (Pagonis, 1992). Subsequent military engagements have also required critical attention to logistical activities.

During the 1960s and 1970s, the impact of global competition on U.S. firms was significant. Companies were losing market share and revenues to firms from other countries, particularly Japan and Germany. Competitive pressures increased in the mid 1970s as trade barriers were reduced, forcing U.S. firms to improve the quality of their products and services, focus on higher levels of customer service and satisfaction, and reduce costs. The amount spent on logistics was identified as the final frontier for cost reduction and improved customer service (Heskett, 1977). Businesses turned their attention to the physical distribution of goods and materials for improved customer service and cost savings. They moved toward logistics management, the integration of transportation, distribution, warehousing, finished goods, inventory management, packaging, and materials handling. Deregulation of transportation played a large part, as increased competition among carriers resulted in lower transportation rates and better management of inbound transportation.

Beginning in the late 1970s and continuing into the 1980s, physical distribution management expanded to logistics management. This movement led to purchasing's increased involvement in logistical decisions, including transportation management, and was influenced by changes in the manufacturing environment and an increased emphasis on quality (Gentry, 1991). The environment had changed as manufacturers moved to outsourcing a greater percentage of the content of their products to outside suppliers. These suppliers were able to produce parts at a lower cost in part because of their non-union environment and related overhead costs, geographic location, and greater economies of scale due to specializing in a few select items. To replace the benefits of controlling production of all parts, many firms moved to a just-in-time (JIT) manufacturing environment. In essence, JIT involved suppliers delivering parts to manufacturing sites when needed for production and producing goods based on actual customer need rather than forecasts, resulting in lower inventory carrying costs. However, it also meant that relationships between suppliers and transportation carriers needed to be stronger to assure delivery within tight windows. In many instances, companies moved to single-sourcing arrangements. At the same time, the total quality management (TQM) movement was in full force, enabling firms to compete with foreign goods producers. The selection of quality carriers was an important part of the equation because manufacturers had to be assured that goods were moved safely and customers were provided a proper level of service. Once firms reduced the number of carriers in the pool, they focused on developing measures of performance and monitoring carriers more closely. These measures included percentage of on-time shipments, percentage of damaged shipments, and percentage of complete orders shipped.

During the late 1980s and 1990s, the term *supply chain management* emerged and was defined as managing the total flow of goods and information from the supplying agency to the final "customer," realizing that each step in the flow of goods should add value (Ellram & Cooper, 1993). Potential savings within a supply chain was the driving factor behind this new trend. A supply chain has a series of "fixed points"—warehouses, distribution centers, and offices where goods are stored—linked together by transportation. This strategy included the development of partnerships with manufacturers, suppliers, and logistics-related members of the supply chain, including transportation carriers. In particular, shippers would spend more time qualifying their carriers. Carrier strategies that could lead to more successful relationships within the supply chain (Wagner & Frankel, 2000), included:

- Partnerships in which both shipper and carrier challenge each other to provide innovative solutions;
- Working jointly with shippers to control transportation costs;
- Providing services considered the highest priority by the shipper;
- Committing to continuous improvement processes that are critical to positive change;
- Implementing satellite communication systems; and
- Providing information systems, logistics consulting, and specialized services based on customer needs.

Transportation Statistics

Logistics costs as a percentage of the gross domestic product (GDP) have continued to drop with the advent of deregulation. At a high of 17.9% in the early 1980s, costs have averaged approximately 10% since 1992 and were 10.1% in 2000 (Cooke, 2001). Freight transportation costs have remained fairly stable over the past 15 years with costs hovering around 6% of the GDP. The most recent figures indicate that in the year 2000, 5.9% of the GDP was accounted for by freight transportation costs, or $590 billion, and is the largest component of logistics costs.

A more complete picture of logistics costs is provided in Figure 1, which breaks down where organizations spent their logistics dollars in 2000. Shippers primarily spent the majority of their dollars (58.2%) on transportation, using trucking as their primary mode. Second in importance were carrying costs, which included interest, taxes, insurance, obsolescence, depreciation, and warehousing.

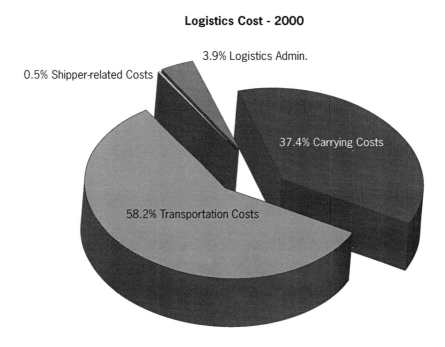

Logistics Cost - 2000

3.9% Logistics Admin.

0.5% Shipper-related Costs

37.4% Carrying Costs

58.2% Transportation Costs

Figure 1. *Logistics costs—2000.*

Source: Cooke, J. A. (2001, July). Steering through the storm. *Logistics Management.*

Figures are also available on actual expenditures by the Federal Government, which support the United States' transportation infrastructure. As shown in Figure 2, the two largest expenditures are highway and air transportation, although they have remained fairly flat in the past few years. Highway expenditures should come as no surprise, given the amount spent by organizations on trucking shipments. The money spent to support rail, water, and city transit has been relatively flat, and funds on developing new pipelines are very limited.

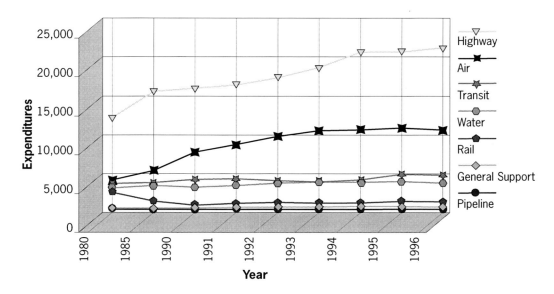

Figure 2. *Federal transportation-related expenditures.*

Transportation Trends

Transportation has played an important role in the development of the United States and, thus, our economy. City locations and their growth were often influenced by access to transportation. For example, Boston initially grew because of its origin as a port city; Chicago was a hub for the railroads; and Atlanta, initially a railroad stop, now has the world's largest airport for passenger service, while Memphis is the largest for cargo transit.

Today, significant changes are occurring within the industry itself. A formerly heavily regulated industry now has the freedom to set prices, determine where they want to operate or discontinue service, and negotiate special services for customers. Cavinato (2001) suggests watching for certain trends in the next 10 years, including:

- Continuing turnover of truckload motor carriers;
- More rail mergers with few capacity changes;
- Consolidation of courier and express mail firms;
- Airline volatility, including bankruptcies and mergers;
- More extensive use of electronic information to provide inventory visibility and efficient billing and payment; and
- Industry consolidation that allows more one-stop shopping.

Wood and Johnson (1995) also foresee an increase of environmental protection and safety laws. Additionally, the impact of recycling on transportation will be significant because packaging choices will be based on potential reuse. Recycled materials and products mean additional hauls for transportation carriers. Finally, threats of terrorism will have a major impact on international trade and transportation carriers. The new challenge will be to reduce time and costs, given the increased security measures taken by the U.S. government. Given these trends, transportation and logistics will continue to be a dynamic and challenging part of the public procurement process.

Conclusion

This chapter introduced the subject of logistics and transportation through definitions of several transportation terms, a short history of the evolution of logistics into its present form today, some important statistics, and current trends for the next ten years. Transportation will continue to grow in the aviation and trucking sectors, while there will be a decline for the railroads. New opportunities will continue for third-party logistics providers who offer several services related to transportation.

References

Cavinato, J. L. (2001, October). Buying transportation today. *Purchasing Today*, 16-18.

Cooke, J. A. (2001, July). Steering through the storm. *Logistics Management*.

Coyle, J. J., Bardi, E. J., & Langley, C. J., Jr. (1996). *The management of business logistics* (6th ed.). Minneapolis/St. Paul, MN: West Publishing Company.

Ellram, L. M., & Cooper, M. C. (1993). Characteristics of supply chain management and the implications for purchasing and logistics strategy. *International Journal of Logistics Management, 4*(2), 13-24.

Gentry, J. J. (1991). *Purchasing's involvement in transportation decision making.* Tempe, AZ: Center for Advanced Purchasing Studies.

Gourdin, K. N. (2001). *Global logistics management.* Oxford, UK: Blackwell Publishers, Ltd.

Heizer, J., & Render, B. (2001). *Principles of operations management.* Upper Saddle River, NJ: Prentice Hall.

Heskett, J. L. (1977, November/December). Logistics—Essential to strategy. *Harvard Business Review.* 84-95.

National Institute of Governmental Purchasing, Inc. (NIGP) (2000). *Intermediate public procurement* (2nd ed.). Herndon, VA: NIGP.

Pagonis, W. G. (1992). *Moving mountains: Lessons in leadership and logistics from the Gulf War.* Boston, MA: Harvard Business School Publishing.

Stock, J. R. (1988). The maturing of transportation: An expanded role for freight carriers. *Journal of Business Logistics, 9*(2), 15-31.

Tzu, S., & Gagliardi, G. (1999). *The art of war: In Sun Tzu's own words.* Seattle, WA: Clearbridge Publishing.

Wagner, W. B., & Frankel, R. (2000). Quality carriers: Critical link in supply chain relationship development. *International Journal of Logistics: Research and Applications, 3*(3), 245-257.

Wood, D. F., & Johnson, J. C. (1995) *Contemporary transportation* (5th ed.). Upper Saddle River, NJ: Prentice Hall

Chapter 2

Transportation Law

The U.S. government has played a major role in the transportation policies that provide the infrastructure, such as roads, bridges, canals, ports, airports, and rights-of-way. It also manages traffic through road safety regulations or rules enforced by the Federal Aviation Administration (FAA) to provide a smooth flow of air traffic. Another important influence over the way carriers transport goods has been the degree of regulation. There are actually four ways in which the U.S. government regulates carriers:

- *Economic regulation*, which is related to the rates carriers can charge;

- *Service regulation*, which ensures that carriers provide services consistent within their operating rights;

- *Safety regulation*, such as drug testing, which falls under the Department of Transportation (DOT) and Occupational Safety and Health Administration (OSHA); and

- *Environmental regulation*, which is the most recent form and affects things such as disposal of municipal and industrial wastes.

Why this degree of regulation? The government wants to ensure the economic development of transportation, i.e., promoting transportation to the public. It wants to protect the public's interest. DOT is responsible for securing our national defense in times of emergency, which means that forms of transportation will be needed to deploy either military equipment or troops to areas as needed. As recently as the Afghanistan conflict, commercial airlines have made pilots and airplanes available to the military for support. One goal of the government is to ensure that all carriers operate fairly and do not discriminate. Transportation laws still include the "common carrier obligation," which states that common carriers (those classified as providing service to all within a certain area) are obligated to provide:

- *Service*: serve all customers who request their service;
- *Delivery*: delivery of goods, with reasonable dispatch, in the same condition as when the carrier picked them up;
- *Reasonable rates*; and
- *Fair treatment*: avoidance of discrimination and treating all customers, products, and geographic locations the same.

Because some of these regulations are still being utilized, it is important to have some understanding of the legislation proposed or enacted over the past 140 years.

History of Transportation Regulation

Railroads

Regulation of the transportation industry was initiated as a result of abuses of economic power in the railroad industry beginning in the 1860s. While railroads had been around for many years along the East Coast, the lure of the West was great for both entrepreneurs and the government. Industrialists wanted to increase their wealth through access to the West's natural resources, such as gold, silver, and lumber. The Federal Government wanted control of California during the Civil War to gain an advantage over the Confederacy. Railroad transportation was the most efficient and available means to link the East with the West.

The U.S. Government passed the Pacific Railroad Act in 1862, which granted public land, known as land grants, to the Union Pacific Railroad for every mile of track laid from Nebraska to California. Others railroads, realizing an opportunity for federal funding, soon started competing with Union Pacific for these land grants. From 1862 to 1871, more than 100 million acres of land was granted to private railroad companies. Railroads became the most important service during the late 1800s and early 1900s, surpassing the use of waterways (West's Legal Directory, n.d., www.wld.com/conbus/weal/wrailrd.htm).

Regulation of the railroads did not begin until 1877, following extensive abuse of the railroads' monopoly of power after the Civil War. Small towns, in particular, were suffering from high rates. The railroads were also offering better rates to their favorite customers, which included those who monopolized the coal, steel, and iron markets. Rebates of 50% to 80% of the published rate to favored shippers were not uncommon, forcing out competitors who were paying higher rates. Another common practice among the railroads was bribery of those in power, such as judges, senators, and governors, to assure that these common abuses of power continued.

Finally, the railroads were manipulating their stock and bond prices. To finance construction of railroad tracks and equipment, they sold stock at inflated prices to unwary investors. This scheme involved "construction companies" that were created and owned by the railroads, which overestimated the costs of construction. These estimates were used to justify stock prices to investors. Investments were sold to unwary investors at rates equal to the inflated costs of construction. Investor funds were then deposited with the construction company, which subcontracted the work to others at actual cost with any differences pocketed by the railroad.

...the Supreme Court ruled that state governments could regulate... interstate railroad rates.

Several Midwestern states responded by passing "granger" laws, which regulated transportation within their states. These laws were contested in several cases and reached the U.S. Supreme Court. In *Munn v. Illinois* (1877), the Supreme Court ruled that state governments could regulate rates "affected with the public interest," i.e., states could regulate interstate railroad rates. (Interstate rates refer to rates charged for freight moved between states, while intrastate rates are rates charged for freight movements within one state.) However, in the Wabash case (1886) (formerly known as Wabash, St. Louis and Pacific Railroad Company v. Illinois), the Supreme Court determined that states could not regulate the intrastate portion of interstate shipments, but required federal action. As a result, Congress passed the Act to Regulate Commerce (1887). Key elements of the law included:

- All interstate or foreign railroad service fell under federal regulation.
- The Interstate Commerce Commission (ICC) was created to administer the law, which included interpretation of the law, rate-setting and issuing mandates.
- Common carrier obligations now fell under the jurisdiction of the ICC.
- Rates had to be "reasonable and just."
- Rate discrimination was outlawed.
- Joint ratemaking among railroads was legal.

Through this Act, carriers were allowed to jointly establish prices for a specific region or geographic area through "rate bureaus," which were organizations maintained by common carriers. The railroads actually supported regulation because competition was increasing, and they wanted to prevent their rates from dropping further.

Major transportation legislation occurred again in the early 1900s, broadening the base of power of the ICC with initial passage of the Elkins Anti-Rebating Act (1903). This act made rates published by the ICC the "official" rates. The Hepburn Act (1906) gave the ICC broader powers to review rate complaints and replace an existing rate with one deemed reasonable and just; however, the ICC remained aligned with the basic rate structure already in place.

This Act also regulated oil pipelines, an emerging mode of transportation, under the Act to Regulate Commerce. The Mann-Elkins Act (1910) gave the ICC new powers to suspend rate increases for up to 10 months while they ran any type of investigation. This Act was the result of the railroad industry's attempt to raise rates to improve profitability. However, realizing that railroads were in financial straits following World War I, Congress passed the Transportation Act of 1920, allowing the ICC to prescribe minimum rates.

The Great Depression of the 1930s led to even more financial problems for the railroads, due to reduced demand and increased competition from motor carriers. In 1933, the Emergency Railroad Transportation Act was passed, which created a Federal Transportation Coordinator to oversee the industry. The Transportation Coordinator did not do much to improve the industry, but his reports to Congress led to the Motor Carrier Act of 1935.

No further railroad regulation occurred until the 1970s. At that time, the railroads were in serious financial condition, and only two major carriers were profitable at the time. Several railroads in the Northeast filed for receivership, which was blamed on too much regulation. Congress initially passed the Regional Rail Reorganization (3-R) Act in 1973, creating the United States Railway Association, which was charged with restructuring the bankrupt railroads. The Consolidated Rail Corporation (Conrail), a semi-public company, was also formed to manage the restructured railroad system. A second act, the Railroad Revitalization and Regulatory Reform Act (4R Act), was passed in 1976.

Motor Carriage

The invention of the automobile led to a new form of competition and threat to the railroads—motor carriage. Between 1914 and 1931, the railroad industry filed multiple lawsuits against trucking firms and applied pressure to state legislatures, resulting in state regulation of trucks and buses. However, the Supreme Court ruled in the 1920s that states could not regulate interstate transportation. In an attempt to restrict competition and avoid federal regulation, motor carriers banded together and developed their own rules of good conduct, which was legal at the time under the National Industrial Recovery Act. Nevertheless, the Supreme Court ruled the Act unconstitutional in the early 1930s. Up to this point, the trucking industry had opposed regulation; but, to protect itself, it changed its position, and Congress passed the Motor Carrier Act of 1935.

Under this Act, the motor carrier industry and brokers were now placed within the oversight of the ICC. Five types of service were recognized—common, contract, private, exempt, and brokerage. As in the railroad industry, common carriers served the general public and charged according to published rates, known as *tariffs*. Contract carriers could negotiate a contract rate with shippers on an individual basis. Private carriers owned the goods they moved and were not for hire to others. Exempt carriers, for-hire transportation companies moving goods not subject to economic regulation, were still required to meet safety standards. Brokers acted as third parties by arranging for and selling transportation services for carriers. To control market entry, common carriers were now required to possess a *certificate of operating rights*, stating the authorized routes they could serve. New carriers were also required to carry a *certificate of public convenience*, and limitations could be placed on a carrier based on their documentation of previous service. All rates had to be filed with the ICC 30 days prior to their effective date, and tariffs were published and made available to all. Proposed tariffs had to cover the full costs of transportation, according to ICC estimates, or were rejected. An exemption was allowed for trucks carrying agricultural products.

If a common carrier was in operation as of June 1, 1935, they were "grandfathered" in, i.e., allowed to continue to serve existing routes. However, their expansion of authority was limited. Only if a route was not already served would the ICC consider extending a license. The purpose of this clause was to prevent new competitors from entering a route already served by existing carrier(s). The end result was the buying and selling of rights to routes from existing carriers. It also created inefficiencies. If Carrier A had the authority to move freight from City A to City B and purchased rights to move freight from City B to City C, Carrier A was required to carry goods originating from City A, bound for City C through City B, even if a shorter route existed between City A and City C.

The Transportation Act of 1958 extended motor carrier regulation to include frozen foods. This Act also contained a National transportation policy directing the ICC to be fair and impartial in its regulation of all modes and "recognize and preserve the inherent advantages of each (mode)." In other words, the ICC should not allow any mode to be driven out of a market.

Airlines

Air travel was also on the upswing with the invention of aircraft large enough to move people and freight. With the passage of the Air Commerce Act of 1926, a central piece of legislation for airline regulation, the Department of Commerce was given authority to regulate air commerce, air traffic, and air safety.

During the period from 1927 to 1938, the airline industry experienced substantial growth. As a result, they were seeking federal aid and protection from "excessive competition." The Air Transport Association (ATA), a trade group, was created in 1936 and helped develop the Civil Aeronautics Act of 1938 to regulate fares, routes, and new entry. Regulation of airways transferred to the Civil Aeronautics Authority (CAA).

The Transportation Act of 1940 included changes in the airline industry. Regulatory authority over airlines was split between the CAA, which would regulate air traffic and air safety enforcement, and the Civil Aeronautics Board (CAB), which is now given the authority to set safety rules, investigate accidents, and regulate economics. However, the Transportation Act of 1958 transferred the duties of the CAA to a newly created agency, the Federal Aviation Agency (FAA).

Water Carriage

The Shipping Act of 1916 was passed, creating the U.S. Shipping Board, whose mission was to stabilize the ocean carrier industry. No other major legislation affecting water transportation was passed until the Transportation Act of 1940, which placed domestic water carriers under ICC rate and service regulation. Exemptions were allowed for those carriers moving three or fewer dry-bulk commodities on one barge or several barges tied together, or movements of liquid bulk products (which covered about 90% of all domestic water shipments).

The Federal Maritime Commission (FMC) was created in 1961 to regulate overseas shipping and investigate practices of ocean carriers and freight operators. It reviews tariff publications under the Shipping Act of 1916.

By the 1970s, the evidence was mounting against continued regulation of motor and air transportation.

Other Major Regulatory Legislation

Freight forwarders consolidate small shipments from several shippers into truckload (TL) or rail car load (CL) lots, and deliver them to carriers for shipment. The Freight Forwarder Act of 1942 added freight forwarders to the list of those covered under federal regulation, stating that they were subject to the Interstate Commerce Act. In effect, entry control, rate, and service requirements were regulated. Freight forwarders could not own and/or control any railroad, oil pipeline, motor carrier, or water carrier, but they could own and/or control other freight forwarders.

The Reed-Bulwinkle Act of 1948 created a new layer of regulation for common carriers by authorizing the use of rate bureaus for all land common carriers. Rate bureaus set rates, but carriers also had the right to establish their own rates if they did not want to participate. Rate bureaus were exempt from antitrust laws.

Impact of Regulation

By the 1970s, the evidence was mounting against continued regulation of motor and air transportation. First, there were significant costs attached to regulation in terms of empty backhauls for motor carriers because routes and products were narrowly specified. Truckers authorized to carry products one way might not be authorized to carry any products on their return trip—the backhaul—resulting in costs attached to moving an empty truck and no offsetting revenue. Second, there were often significant differences in trucking rates between movements of exempt products and near-equivalent regulated products. For example, the variation in tariffs between uncooked and cooked poultry was 50% (Moore, 1995). As a result, the share of total traffic carried by exempt carriers had increased not only because of lower rates but because exempt carriers were better able to meet shippers' needs. Finally, union workers in both the motor carrier and airline industries had negotiated large pay increases on a regular basis, which added to the cost of transportation.

Several other factors forced Congress to repeal much of the regulation over these two industries. Ralph Nader, a young activist at the time, and his "Nader's Raiders" were visibly critical of regulatory agencies. A national fuel crisis also resulted in scrutiny of the transportation industry's excessive fuel consumption and lead Congress to the conclusion that regulatory policies were at fault. University economists had been strongly opposed to regulation of the trucking industry as early as 1928, and their opposition continued into the late 1970s. They argued that under competitive pricing, rates would be driven down, whereas regulation meant carriers would always force rates up to meet costs. With regulation, they argued, there was no reason to contain costs.

DOT, Congress, and the Department of Justice were strongly in favor of truck deregulation; and, as a result, the National Transportation Policy Study Commission (an independent commission) was formed. Their findings resulted in a recommendation that regulatory reform be made a priority item. Although the ICC initially took the position that regulation was needed to ensure a stable industry, it began a series of reforms on its own after Congressional and public debates.

The trucking industry as a whole and the Teamsters in particular were against deregulation. The Teamsters realized that deregulation would lessen their power and result in fewer union jobs. However, different transportation interest groups favored certain reforms. Large shippers were generally in favor of deregulation, but smaller shippers and rural areas were against it because of worries over loss of service.

With several railroads in the Northeast in bankruptcy, changes to the laws regarding the railroads were prompted by concerns over future viability of the industry. Congress realized that changes were occurring in the marketplace: (a) most transportation in the United States was already very competitive; (b) government regulation, for the most part, had become unnecessary and inefficient; (c) most intercity freight was transported by modes other than rail; and (d) railroad earnings were the lowest of all modes and insufficient to make needed capital improvements to survive (Sampson, Farris, & Shrock, 1981). As a result, it was determined that new legislation was needed.

The push for economic deregulation of the airlines came with the appointment of Alfred E. Kahn to chairman of the Civil Aeronautics Board (CAB). An economist, his mission was to eliminate all regulation. At that time, airfares were high, which limited access and choices to the general public.

Deregulation of the Transportation Industry

Airlines

While much of the national debate centered on the trucking industry, the first mode deregulated was the airline industry. In 1976, the CAB started loosening restrictions on the airlines, which were accelerated under Alfred E. Kahn as CAB chairman. President Carter signed the Airline Deregulation Act in 1978, which instructed the CAB to focus on regulatory decisions that advocated competition while preserving service to small communities. Airlines were now automatically allowed to enter into markets served by the competition. Fares were no longer regulated, and airlines were not required to file rate changes. Discount fares were allowed for the first time. The legislation also included a "sunset clause" for the CAB, requiring them to disband by January 1, 1985.

In 1978, the ICC also took several actions, including:

- Applying city rates to larger areas and expanding carrier authority for pickup and delivery;
- Enlarging airport zones to give airline trucks expanded areas for pickup and delivery;
- Allowing railroads to enter into contracts with shippers;
- Eliminating economic regulation for railroads on perishable farm produce;
- Granting requests for operating authority for most motor carriers; and
- Allowing private truckers to apply for operating authority as common or contract carriers on their backhauls.

Motor Carrier Act of 1980

The trucking industry was deregulated but not as extensively as the airline industry. Market entry was opened to any carrier that could prove its financial ability to take on an operation, i.e., be fit, willing, and able, and verify that the proposed service would serve a useful purpose. A Master Certificate System was created in which any carrier deemed fit, willing, and able would automatically be granted a certificate for any community not regularly served by a common carrier. Certificates applied to U.S. government freight, vehicles for small packages (i.e., less than 100 lbs.), and owner-operated vehicles for food and edible products if the tonnage did not exceed that of exempt products. To protect shippers, all carriers would now be required to carry at least $75,000 of insurance, and requirements were made higher if the carrier moved hazardous materials.

Controls on rates were loosened with the creation of a "zone of rate freedom." Carriers were now allowed to increase/decrease rates by 10% each year without approval of the ICC and an additional 5% at the discretion of the ICC. After two years, changes in rates would be tied to the producers' price index (PPI). Carriers could discuss and vote on general rate increases but not single-line rate proposals.

The distinctions among classes of carriers also blurred. Contract carriers, previously limited to a maximum of eight customers, were no longer given limits. Additionally, private carriers could now carry freight for wholly-owned subsidiaries of the same corporation. Further, to alleviate the backhaul problem, the number of products classified as "exempt" was expanded. This clause improved backhaul opportunities for those carriers primarily moving agricultural products to market.

As a result, there was a significant increase in the number of small interstate motor carriers. Approximately half of all TL carriers filed bankruptcy between 1980 and 1989; but since then, the market has been fairly stable. Rates declined approximately 25% from 1977 to 1983 and contributed to the number of bankrupt carriers. Service levels have increased; but, as predicted by the unions, there has been a significant increase of non-union workers.

In 1995, Congress completed deregulation of the trucking industry through the Federal Aviation Administration Authorization Act of 1994, eliminating state regulation of intrastate trucking rates. However, some groups are still excluded from deregulation, including buses, household goods movers, and garbage haulers.

Maislin v. Primary Steel

Because of changes in control over rates and a surge in competition, motor carriers often negotiated rates far below the published tariffs to gain business, but never filed these rates with the ICC. Millions of dollars in undercharges (the difference between the negotiated and published rates) were discovered during financial audits of multiple trucking firms. As a result, carriers now in bankruptcy attempted to collect these undercharges, and eventually the legality of this practice was tested before the Supreme Court in 1990. In *Maislin v. Primary Steel* (1989), the court upheld the "filed rate doctrine" of the Elkins Act of 1903, which stated that common carrier negotiated rates were legal only if published in a tariff by the ICC.

The Negotiated Rates Act of 1993 (NRA) was an outcome of the Supreme Court's decision. Under the Act, shippers would now have the option of settling undercharges by paying 15% of the claim amount on TL shipments (greater than 10,000 lbs.) or 20% on less-than-truckload (LTL) shipments to the party that claims it was damaged by the undercharges. Finally, in 1994, the Trucking Industry Regulatory Reform Act (TIRRA) was passed, eliminating the filing requirements for common carriers using individually determined rates versus bureau-set rates. Individually determined rates are those set by one carrier for service provided on its own line. Carriers must keep a list of these individual tariffs and provide them to any existing or potential shipper upon request. The "filed rate doctrine" remains law to this day.

Sunset of ICC

The ICC was eliminated by the ICC Termination Act of 1995. Transportation regulation was placed with the Surface Transportation Board (STB) under the Department of Transportation (DOT). The ICC Termination Act and TIRRA resulted in elimination of the distinction between common and contract carriers. Tariff filing and rate regulations were repealed with the exception of household goods movements or those affecting noncontiguous domestic trade. The STB has broad exemption authority over cargo loss and damage, insurance, safety fitness, and antitrust immunity, while registration of motor carriers now falls under the DOT. Certificates of operating authority are no longer required. A carrier must prove safety fitness and financial responsibility only.

Railroad Legislation

The Railroad Revitalization and Regulatory Reform Act, better known as the 4-R Act, was passed in 1976. The purpose of the Act was twofold—to rescue the railroad industry in the Northeast and to reform past regulation. Changing demographics in the Northeast had resulted in excess rail capacity and a greater need for short-haul movements. The railroads' cost structure was high because of expensive labor contracts and track repair. As a result, freight rates were high. Several railroads had already filed for bankruptcy. The first part of the Act created the United States Railway Association with the responsibility of planning and financing the restructuring of these bankrupt railroads. Conrail was created to operate the restructured railroad system.

Regulatory reforms included the establishment of a zone of rate freedom, which allowed railroads to raise or lower rates without prior ICC approval by 7% from beginning-of-the-year rates if they did not "dominate" the market. A railroad was considered to dominate the market if one of the following conditions existed: (a) the carrier controlled at least 70% of the traffic; (b) the proposed rate was at least 160% or more of the carrier's variable costs; or (c) shippers were locked into shipping with the carrier because of substantial investment in the carrier's facilities. Rates equal to or greater than variable costs could not be considered "too low" and, thus, were reasonable. However, no rate could be considered "too high" by the ICC unless it was determined that the railroad dominated that particular market. The ICC was required to shorten the length of time taken to make decisions on proposals, such as rates changes or mergers.

The Staggers Rail Act of 1980 followed, continuing a focus on improving the financial viability of the railroads. It was a long and complicated 78-page document with 61 sections. The definition of "market dominance" was specified as 160% of variable costs in 1981 but increasing by 5% per year until 1984 to a maximum of 180%. A centerpiece of the Act was creating a "zone of rate flexibility" to increase a carrier's freedom in setting rates. If rates were greater than a carrier's variable costs, they could adjust their rates equal to inflation plus 6%, with a maximum of 18% until l984. After January 1984, carriers could increase rates by inflation plus 4% per year if the railroad had market dominance. Maximum rates were no longer subject to ICC controls if the railroad did not have "market dominance," i.e., situations where the railroad controlled the market or where rates exceed 160% of variable costs. Rates could then be set freely. However, if they did possess market dominance, the ICC could regulate rates when they appeared to exceed 160% of variable costs. Contract rates were legalized. Railroads could now contract with shippers for up to 40% of their capacity, although contracts had to be filed and approved by the ICC. Shippers could protest rates but were limited to allegations that rates would impair the railroad's ability to serve other shippers. Competing carriers cannot oppose contracts. With the ICC Termination Act of 1995, railroad mergers are now reviewed by the STB. Tariff filings and most contract filings for carriers have been eliminated. However, any rate increases or changes in service must be filed with 20 days' advance notice.

By deregulating fares and routes, competition was expected to increase and result in lower fares.

In summary, the objectives of deregulation varied depending on the industry. In the case of the airlines, legislation was intended to increase travel opportunities for the general public. By deregulating fares and routes, competition was expected to increase and result in lower fares. The objective of deregulating motor carriers was to improve their operating efficiencies, therefore reducing fuel costs, which was a major concern in the 1970s. Finally, legislation was enacted to improve railroad economic viability. Most would agree that reforms were needed at the time, although the results have not always been positive. While airline fares have indeed decreased, so have service levels. Motor carriers initially faced severe new competition and then fallout as bankruptcy filings increased. Finally, the railroad industry still faces multiple hurdles although motor carriers now rely on them for movement of trailers (trailer on flatcar [TOFC]) and containers (container on flatcar [COFC]).

Federal Transportation Agencies

Established by Congress in 1966, DOT is the agency responsible overall for safety, systems, technology, and mass transit development. Led by the Secretary of Transportation, the DOT "oversees the formulation of National transportation policy and promotes intermodal transportation" (DOT, www.dot/gov/ost/). The DOT has several strategic goals:

- To promote the public health and safety by working toward elimination of transportation-related deaths and injuries;
- To shape an accessible, affordable, reliable transportation system for all people, goods, and regions;

- To support a transportation system that sustains America's growth;

- To protect and enhance communities and the natural environment that is protected by transportation; and

- To ensure the security of the transportation system for the movement of people and goods and support the National Security Strategy. (DOT, www.dot/gov)

With the exception of the U.S. Army Corps of Engineers, the DOT includes 12 federal agencies that promote transportation (Figure 3), the newest of which is the Transportation Security Administration. A brief description of several of those agencies follows.

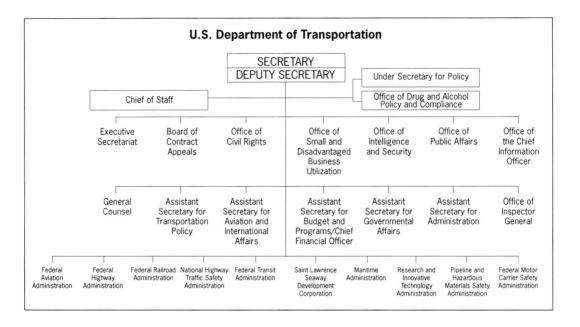

Figure 3. *U.S. Department of Transportation organization chart.*

Source: U.S. Department of Transportation, www.dot.gov.

Federal Aviation Administration (FAA). FAA is primarily responsible for the safety of the aviation system. It rates and certifies pilots as well as the airports. It is charged with regulating a program that ensures security of civil aviation and enforces the regulations of the Hazardous Materials Transportation Act. It operates all airport towers, routes air traffic through its control towers, and develops air traffic rules.

Federal Highway Administration (FHWA). FHWA is responsible for coordinating highway transportation programs within the 50 states. It is comprised of several major programs, including the Federal-Aid Highway Program, which provides financial aid to states for new construction or improvement of highways, roads and bridges. Another program, the Federal Lands Highway Program is responsible for road access into and out of public lands, preparing plans and contracts, developing surveys, supervising construction, and inspecting bridges when necessary.

Federal Railroad Administration (FRA). FRA promotes the safety of rail transportation. Federal safety inspectors monitor the railroads to ensure they follow standards for operating practices and maintenance of tracks. It also provides educational programs to educate the public on railroad crossing safety and the dangers of trespassing on railroad property.

National Highway Traffic Safety Administration (NHTSA). NHTSA is responsible for reducing deaths, injuries and economic losses resulting from motor vehicle crashes. NHTSA sets and enforces safety performance standards for motor vehicles and equipment. NHTSA investigates safety defects in motor vehicles, sets and enforces fuel economy standards, helps states and local communities reduce the threat of drunk drivers, promotes the use of safety belts, child safety seats and air bags, investigates odometer fraud, establishes and enforces vehicle anti-theft regulations and provides consumer information on motor vehicle safety topics.

Federal Transit Administration (FTA). FTA assists in developing improved mass transportation system for cities and communities nationwide. Through its grant programs, FTA helps plan, build, and operate transit systems with convenience, cost and accessibility in mind. In providing financial, technical and planning assistance, the agency provides leadership and resources for safe and technologically advanced local transit systems while assisting in the development of local and regional traffic reduction.

Saint Lawrence Seaway Development Corporation (SLSDC). SLSDC oversees the movement of commercial and noncommercial vessels through the Saint Lawrence Seaway, providing inspection of vessels, navigation aids, and traffic control. It also looks for trade opportunities that could benefit the local community.

Maritime Administration (MARAD). MARAD assures national security and promotes the U.S. shipping industry. It works to ensure competitiveness of the U.S. shipbuilding industry through its subsidy programs for vessel operations. It also works to improve U.S. participation in foreign and domestic trade.

Research & Innovative Technology Administration (RITA). RITA is an agency whose mission is to identify and facilitate solutions to the challenges and opportunities facing America's transportation system. RITA's focus is to promote transportation research that will foster the use of innovative technology. With responsibility for research policy and technology sharing, the agency partners with national and international organizations and universities.

Pipeline and Hazardous Materials Safety Administration (PHMSA). PHMSA oversees the safety of more than 800,000 daily shipments of hazardous materials in the United States and 64 percent of the nation's energy that is transported by pipelines. PHMSA is dedicated solely to safety by working toward the elimination of transportation-related deaths and injuries in hazardous materials and pipeline transportation, and by promoting transportation solutions that enhance communities and protect the natural environment.

Federal Motor Carrier Safety Administration (FMCSA). Established in 2000, FFMCSA is charged with preventing commercial truck-related injuries and fatalities. Their purview includes (a) enforcement of safety regulations; (b) improvement of safety information systems; (c) strengthening of standards; and (d) increasing safety awareness.

Conclusions

The government has been heavily involved in ensuring economically viable and safe transportation systems. Initially, the role of the government was to protect the shipper through regulation. Later, the government continued regulation as a means to protect various modes of transportation from competition. Today, we face a largely deregulated environment, which began in the late 1970s. The Department of Transportation, with its various programs, remains in place to promote private transportation to the public, regulate the safety of all modes, and ensure the continuation of our infrastructure through subsidies and construction of highways, airports, and bridges.

References

Moore, T. G. (1995). Clearing the track: The remaining transportation regulations. *Regulation,* 18(2).

Sampson, R. J., Farris, M. T., & Shrock, D. L. (1985). *Domestic transportation: Practice, theory, and policy.* Boston, MA: Houghton Mifflin Company.

Chapter 3

Mode And Carrier Selection

The means by which a purchased item is brought into an organization as a result of an acquisition is frequently overlooked, e.g., computer hardware. The focus of attention is on the solicitation method or contract type, but issues of delivery are an afterthought. The importance of determining the mode of transportation is an essential step in the government procurement process and cannot be overlooked.

Certainly, there are transportation means that are more common than others in the public sector. Having goods shipped via the ground freight carrier determined by the supplier is a common approach, but there are a number of other tools available for today's government buyer, such as air freight, bus service, rail car, water carriers, and pipelines. With all of these logistical options, the public buyer is challenged with making the right determination for the particular purchase. Whether or not the delivery services should be purchased separately is another decision that must be made. Will the contract for the purchase of goods also include the transportation? Will the transportation services involve a separate agreement with another supplier? These are fundamental elements of the procurement process.

Along with the choice of transportation mode comes the selection of the carrier that will actually transport the goods. Many companies offer both public and contracted transportation services to their clients. In most transportation industries, this creates a sound, competitive environment, with the selection of the "right" carrier ultimately falling to the procurement professional. This type of challenge is one of the reasons that transportation system selection is viewed as a specialized form of procurement.

Auxiliary services also play a valuable role in transportation. These may include third-party service providers such as freight forwarders and brokers. Depending on the level of expertise within an agency, as well as the staffing capacity, having a third party lend their logistics expertise can be a good investment.

Transportation Modes

Transportation is a complex industry that includes a number of modes, or types of delivery methods. Both public and private buyers have a number of options available to them for transporting goods and materials. The five primary modes of transportation are:

- motor carriage
- air cargo
- pipeline

- rail freight
- water

Each of these modes has its own unique capability, with inherent advantages and disadvantages as shown in Table 1, followed by an overview and analysis of each mode.

Mode	Shipment Types	Advantages	Disadvantages
Motor Carriage	• Parcels • LTL • TL	• Easy accessibility • Reliable service • Fast transit times • Good security	• Impacted by weather • Transit not always smooth • High shipping rates
Rail Freight	• Commodities • CL • LCL • Containers • Trailers	• Move large volumes • Low cost • Unaffected by weather	• Limited accessibility • Long transit times
Air Cargo	• Documents • Parcels • Containers	• Fast delivery times • Smooth transit	• High shipping rates • Limited accessibility
Water	• Commodities • Equipment • Containers	• Ideal for bulk material • Support global trade	• Limited accessibility • Long transit times • Lower reliability
Pipeline	• Bulk	• Dependable transit times • Unaffected by weather	• Initial investment costly • Limited to certain materials

Table 1. *Comparison of Transportation Modes: Advantages and Disadvantages*

Motor Carriage

The dominant mode of transportation is motor carriage, or trucking. In 2000, approximately $481 billion was spent in the United States alone, accounting for more than 80% of all transportation revenue generated. This industry consists of a large number of small motor carriers, which results in a very high level of competition. Public and private organizations use this mode extensively because of high availability, ease of accessibility, relatively fast transit times, and a level of service that is generally reliable. The motor carrier industry has two roughly equal segments—*for-hire* and *private carriages*. *For-hire* carriage, moved by the truckload (TL), accounts for 95% of the activity, with less-than-truckload (LTL) accounting for the remaining 5% (WEFA-DRI, 2001c). The average truckload delivery spans about 350 miles with market dominance continuing up to 750 miles. Trucks move such items as raw materials, component parts, and finished goods. Trucking companies also support the rail industry, often loading their trailers onto rail cars for transport. Other motor carriers include parcel delivery services, such as the United Parcel Service (UPS) and Federal Express (FedEx). These privately owned carriers provide package delivery services for many government organizations. Items such as repair parts and office supplies are commonly transported in this way due to competitive pricing and strong commitment to service.

The question often arises as to who is responsible for the loading and unloading of an LTL shipment. According to the National Motor Freight Classification (NMFC), those responsibilities are clearly spelled out in *Item 58:*

> *Heavy or Bulky Freight-Loading or Unloading.* When a freight container weighs less than 110 pounds, the carrier will perform both the loading and the unloading. For freight packages or pieces over 500 pounds, the consignor is required to perform the loading and the consignee the unloading. The truck driver may assist with loading or unloading upon request. When it comes to freight between 110 and 500 pounds, the driver's responsibility depends on whether the consignor (sender) or consignee (receiver) provides an accessible dock or ramp. Again, upon request, the truck driver may assist with the loading and unloading. (Bohman, 2002)

Within the motor carrier industry, there are four basic types of carriers (Coyle, Bardi, & Langley, 1996). The majority of industrial freight is transported by common carriers, which offer the transportation of goods to any shipper based on published tariffs that must be reasonable and nondiscriminatory to the shipper. Tariffs are based on a classification system, or grouping of products, based on similar transportation characteristics. Contract carriers are somewhat different from common carriers in that they operate under set contractual agreements with designated customers rather than the general public (although these lines have blurred since deregulation). The services can be tailored to meet the specialized needs of the shipper, providing special equipment or arranging for customized pick-up and delivery schedules. Exempt carriers make up a third category, so-called because they are exempt from economic regulation of rates and services. The marketplace determines their rates. Exempt carriers are limited to the movement of agricultural products, newspapers, livestock, and fish. The fourth category is the private carrier, which involves transportation of materials with trucks and equipment owned by an agency or company. Private carriers are not "for-hire" and are exempt from federal economic regulation, e.g., electrical supply houses and governments that handle their own transportation.

Although air freight has made significant inroads into the trucking share of transportation, trucks still account for 70% of small package shipments. In 1999 alone, the top 100 trucking firms reported revenue of just under $70 billion. The future looks generally bright for this industry with continued growth expected in the coming years. Along with this growth, there will be consolidations of TL and LTL carriers as well as outsourcing by private fleets (WEFA-DRI, 2001c).

Rail Freight

There are eight large railroads, referred to as *Class I* carriers, in the United States, with more than 500 additional small operators. Class I railroads earn in excess of $266 million per year. Although Canada does not use the class system, Canadian National Railroad and Canadian Pacific Railroad would also qualify as Class I carriers.

Class I carriers account for approximately 9% of revenue generated by all modes, moving about 25% of all freight tonnage (WEFA, 2001b). Coal, grain, metallic ores, crushed stone, and glass and clay products are commodities that are commonly carried on railroads. All railroads are considered common carriers, with the legal responsibility to serve all customers at reasonable prices without discrimination.

One of the prime advantages of rail transport is the ability to move large volumes of all types of commodities over a great distance with a relatively low cost structure. Similar to the trucking industry, rail shipments move in full carload (CL) as well as less-than-carload (LCL) shipments. A significant disadvantage is the limited access provided by the railways, which results in the need for additional transportation modes to complete deliveries. Another disadvantage is the long transit time due to the consolidation and transfer of boxcars at yards within the rail system. However, rail service remains a viable means of transportation. The reliability and dependability of rail transport is higher than other modes because it is generally unaffected by poor weather.

One of the prime advantages of rail transport is the ability to move large volumes of all types of commodities over a great distance with a relatively low cost structure.

With the trucking industry remaining one of the largest customers of rail, it will continue to be a formidable player in transportation. In 2002, it was expected that railroad commodity loadings would increase by 1.2%. Through the next decade, rail transportation will continue to benefit from growth in foreign trade, which translates into healthy increases in rail intermodal traffic (WEFA-DRI, 2001b).

Air Cargo

In 2000, a total of $27 billion was spent on international and domestic air freight. That amount is still considered relatively small in the transportation market. The movement of goods through the air has certainly increased in recent years, but the relatively high cost has kept its use limited within government spending trends.

As a general rule of thumb, the freight rates for air cargo are approximately twice as high as motor freight. However, along with the higher costs are certain advantages. Because air travel is usually much smoother than ground transportation, it is very attractive for transporting delicate equipment (National Institute of Governmental Purchasing, Inc. [NIGP], 2000). Another advantage is the shorter delivery times involved with air transport. A specialized repair part, for instance, can be shipped from New York to California in one day, with many commercial companies providing such service. Since typical motor carrier delivery would take several days, the option to use air freight becomes that much more attractive. With shorter lead times for products, organizations can normally reduce their inventories on hand as well as their carrying costs.

During the 1990s, air cargo experienced phenomenal growth, with ton-miles increasing by 88%. Even with this growth, it still accounts for a very small percentage of intercity transportation. Throughout the next decade, air-ton miles are expected to rise at a rate of 6.5% to 7% per year (WEFA-DRI, 2001a).

Water

Water transportation plays a significant role in logistics spending, accounting for $26 billion of total logistics dollars spent within the United States. This mode is frequently used by organizations located in strategic areas to move raw materials, heavy items, and low-value bulk materials. Road salt is one example of a common government commodity that is often transported by water. Water carriers, the oldest method of transportation, include barges used on inland waterways and ocean-going ships.

The cost of pickup and delivery of goods to the dockside needs to be included in the total cost of shipping, as these costs are not included in water freight rates. Water carriers normally base their charges on either weight or volume, depending on which one results in the highest revenue for the carrier (NIGP, 2000). The Federal Government has been involved with improving the waterways within the United States for a long time. The U.S. Army Corps of Engineers is the agency that provides oversight and funding for river and harbor improvements, e.g., enlarging docks and deepening channels.

Waterborne commerce will remain a strong force with growth and expansion projected at 2% per year through 2010. Even with such growth, this mode will account for only 11% of the total domestic intercity tonnage. However, by 2010, the total export tonnage in water transport is expected to reach 500 million tons (WEFA-DRI, 2001d).

Pipelines

Pipelines, referred to as the "hidden giant of American transportation," have been around since 1865 when Samuel Van Syckel constructed a five-mile oil pipeline in Pennsylvania (Wood & Johnson, 1995). Along with extensive use in the oil industry, pipelines are also used to transport other materials, such as natural gas and coal slurry. The total transportation costs for oil pipelines alone were $9 billion in 2000. Within the United States, there are over 110 regulated oil pipelines. Since 1977, the Federal Energy Regulatory Commission (FERC) has regulated the oil pipeline industry.

The dependability of this transportation mode is extremely high as far as getting the product to its destination when promised. Because pipelines are virtually unaffected by the weather, they really have no equal when it comes to dependability. One disadvantage to pipeline transportation is the high costs associated with installing and maintaining the piping systems. The material, labor, and equipment costs can be extensive, including such things as specialty piping, journey level labor, pumps, and computerized flow controls. Still, pipelines continue to be a viable means of transportation in the United States, particularly in the oil and natural gas industries.

Intermodal Carriage

Organizations often use more than one mode of transportation to move freight to its destination. *Intermodal carriage*, the use of two or more transportation modes to deliver goods seamlessly to their ultimate destination, fills the gap (Coyle et al., 1996). This combined method of transport surfaced back in the 1800s, when the Long Island Railroad offered to carry farmers' wagons on flat cars bound for New York City (Wood & Johnson, 1995).

Intermodal service may be necessary because of the limits of each individual mode of transportation. For example, air delivery is limited to airports and requires transfer and delivery by landed modes such as rail and motor carriage. Thus, various modes can be combined to overcome their limitations while moving freight at the lowest possible cost. Motor carriage is used frequently in intermodal freight movements due to its high accessibility to destination points.

Intermodal carriage most commonly involves moving loaded trailers or containers from the shipper's facility on one type of carrier and then finishing the journey on another carrier mode. The typical surface container comes in standard sizes of 20 or 40 feet long and 8 feet wide.

Various terms have been created to describe intermodal movements of freight. For example, when shipments are moved from truck tractor to a rail car for long-haul movements, it is referred to as *piggyback*. The term *fishyback* is used when water and motor carriers ship the container, while *birdyback* refers to the freight movement by air and truck. Other combinations are also possible, as shown in Figure 4.

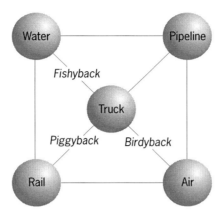

Figure 4. *Intermodal options.*

In the past, transportation regulations in the United States discouraged multimodal transportation companies—those offering more than one type of transportation. Since deregulation, however, the buying market has demanded more efficient and cost-effective transportation, which has helped to bolster the growth of intermodalism (Wood & Johnson, 1995). While carriers were once offering multiple transportation modes to their customers to stay competitive, most have returned to their primary mode and added other services. UPS and FedEx are two notable exceptions, each with a fleet of airplanes and trucks. Partnerships between motor carriers, railroads, or motor carriers and railroads are more commonly negotiated today to improve service and costs to shippers. For example, the Burlington Northern and Santa Fe Railway Company (BNSF) and the Norfolk Southern Railway Company (NS) offer coast-to-coast carload service for temperature-controlled commodities from Washington State cities of Seattle, Tacoma, Yakima, and Pasco to the Midwest, Northeast and Southeast (www.bnsf.com). Intermodal marketing companies (IMCs) have also been created, acting as intermediaries to solicit intermodal traffic for the railroads. With options for integrating multiple modes and providing maximum flexibility, intermodal transportation will continue to benefit global markets and distribution systems. It requires a broader knowledge of transportation processes within the supply chain, as it focuses on a holistic view of transportation (DeWitt & Clinger, 2000).

Carrier Selection

According to Leenders and Flynn (1995), choosing the right supplier can help ensure operational success for an organization. This is certainly the case when purchasing goods, but it can be just as important when it comes to determining how those same goods will be transported to their final destination. While the initial determination made by an organization may very well be mode of delivery, the choice of carriers will certainly be next. It is not difficult to see how important quality and timely goods are to an organization, particularly when one considers the seven "Rights" of customer satisfaction:

- The **Right** product
- Delivered to the **Right** place
- At the **Right** time
- In the **Right** condition and packaging
- In the **Right** quantity
- At the **Right** cost
- To the **Right** customer (Kuglin, 1998).

The importance of quality, accuracy, and timeliness in the delivery of goods is apparent. These factors influence which carrier the procurement professional ultimately selects.

Who Manages the Transportation Decision?

A key consideration for public procurement professionals at all levels is whether or not to buy transportation and delivery services separate from the goods purchase itself. The predominant trend within the public arena is to shift the burden of carrier selection to the supplier. With the goods contract that includes the delivery, (often in the form of a purchase order) the supplier is responsible for determining which carrier will be used.

Even though many government purchases require the supplier to handle carrier selection, there are many instances where it can be beneficial to contract separately for transportation. Many organizations handle the outbound shipping of goods and equipment from their own facilities and contract directly with carriers to transport them. For example, when a water treatment facility needs to ship specialized control equipment to the equipment manufacturer for repair or upgrade, in order to ensure quality transportation of such critical equipment, the organization may likely have a contract already in place with a carrier. The carrier would pick up the equipment at the specified location and then transport it to the manufacturer's facility. Once the needed repairs are completed, the organization would hire the carrier to bring the equipment back for its scheduled installation. This approach can also be viable for incoming freight. Rather than relying on an unknown carrier selected by the supplier, an organization may wish to contract with its own carrier. This offers the public agency more control and oversight during the transportation process and may even result in a lower cost.

Some may feel that it is easier to simply rely on the supplier to select the carrier. This often takes less agency staff time and energy and will likely have favorable results. When a time-critical shipment is needed, most organizations would rather be in control of carrier delivery. Suppliers also determine the cost of transportation, which may not always be to the agency's benefit. Purchasing and supply managers are in the best position to work with their suppliers to keep transportation costs down (Pinkerton & Marien, 1997).

If procurement professionals do decide to contract for transportation services, they will face many of the same issues encountered with other types of services. A determination needs to be made as to which procurement method will be employed. Traditionally, many government services have been awarded through an Invitation for Bids (IFB) process. This solicitation method sets out minimum requirements, with the contract usually going to the bidder providing the lowest price. A Request for Proposal (RFP) process is another option for procurement professionals. An RFP will take into account other aspects of the offer that the organization determines as valuable. These can include service quality, corporate experience, financial stability, customer satisfaction, and prior dealings, among other factors. According to research by McGinnis (1990), service is often more important than cost when selecting transportation carriers.

...service is often more important than cost when selecting transpor-tation carriers.

In contracting for services, including transportation, procurement professionals have several options. Depending upon the contracting rules of the agency, direct negotiations may be appropriate and allowable. As in other procurements, it is the procurement professional's responsibility to help determine the most appropriate means of purchasing. By keeping abreast of current trends and methods, one can draw upon the best solution or practice for a given situation. No single procurement method will fit every need. According the National Association of State Procurement Officials (NASPO) (2001), "It must be recognized that, while the purchase of services requires <u>innovative</u> methods of acquiring quality services at a reasonable price, <u>traditional</u> procurement strategies are amenable to the process" (p. 74).

The current process will probably accommodate techniques for saving money. Regardless of the procurement and contract type utilized, transportation contracts give carriers the opportunity to secure a large volume of business from an organization. Such opportunities normally result in very favorable offers from the carrier community. Additionally, long-term agreements with multi-year options can provide an opportunity for a carrier to become a strategic partner of the public entity. After the contract is executed and the business relationship is formally established, the organization has the ability to utilize the carrier as the need arises. Sound contract documents, frequent communications, and effective contract administration can all contribute to a favorable partnership for both parties. Similar agreements can also be made with third-party providers of transportation services. When a public agency contracts with a freight forwarder or broker, such contractors can provide whatever transportation mode is needed, which offers the buyer greater flexibility.

Auxiliary Service Providers

Most organizations, including state and local governments, utilize outside logistics services to supplement their own workforce. Such efforts allow the procurement professional to fulfill the service delivery needs of their agency. A critical part of their role is to coordinate the flow of goods and services throughout their entity and in support of its objectives. Whether the services are performed internally or externally may be of no consequence to an end-user. If the traffic signal equipment arrives at the project site on time, the needs of the engineer overseeing the intersection project have been met. It is this type of operational contribution that procurement professionals need to concentrate on when evaluating their role within the organization. The outside, auxiliary services can take on a variety of forms.

Third Party Logistics Providers

Third-party logistics providers (sometimes referred to as 3PL) refer to independent companies that design, implement, and/or manage an organization's supply chain logistics needs. A key difference between a 3PL and typical transportation service provider is that the 3PL's value is based on information and knowledge, as opposed to simply providing the same service at a lower cost (Konezny & Beskow, 1999). This is a growing area for organizations of all types. A recent report by Armstrong and Associates (Duffy, 1999) stated that in the United States alone, the total gross revenues for third-party logistics providers exceeded $34 billion, with net revenues growing by 20% each year.

While there may be different levels of use and integration of 3PLs within an agency, some of the most common functions are seen in Table 2. Some of the performance standards that an organization might use with these providers are similar to their own operations. Factors such as inventory accuracy, turnaround time, customer satisfaction, and on-time deliveries are all important.

Service Area	Currently Use	Plan to Use in Future
Outbound Transportation	62.9%	11.8%
Warehousing	62.9%	16.1%
Freight Bill Audit/Payment	53.2%	17.7%
Inbound Transportation	48.9%	15.6%
Freight Distribution	38.2%	19.9%
Information Technology	12.9%	10.8%
Order Fulfillment	9.7%	6.5%
Customer Service	6.5%	8.1%

Table 2. *Outsourced Logistics Services: Current Versus Future Plans*

Source: Ernst & Young. (1999). *Third-party logistics: Views from the customers.* Ernst & Young, Fourth Annual Study. Knoxville: University of Tennessee.

In a 1999 Ernst & Young study, respondents indicated that their organizations either used third-party logistics services or were at least considering their use in the future. Inbound and outbound transportation, warehousing, and distribution seem to be the most commonly used areas, but other functions, such as customer service and information technology, appear to be gaining ground. This means that 3PLs must be able to provide a wide array of services in order to meet this demand, both today and in the future.

Piper Jaffray Equity Research (Konezny & Beskow, 1999) identified five crucial areas that 3PLs must possess in order to offer true value to the public and private organizations that they serve:

- Demonstrated strong core competency and economies of scale;
- Information technology as a key component in their logistics operation;
- Breadth of services; possessing a broader array of services;
- Geographical presence; expertise in foreign markets with global presence; and
- Flexible, performance-driven culture in the work place.

It should be added that a key to successfully working with 3PLs is maintaining a sound relationship with the provider. Developing a sound contractual agreement and a bond of mutual trust can play well for both parties. While it may likely be the financial or executive powers that recognize the need for a 3PL, the organization will certainly rely on the procurement professional when it comes to implementation.

Freight Forwarders

Freight forwarders provide a valuable service by providing transportation to firms with LCL lots. These smaller shipments are combined with other such shipments to make a full load and then transported at the CL rate. Freight forward shipments normally move more quickly than ordinary LCL shipments if the traveling distance is over 300 miles. The rates are quite competitive. In nearly all cases, freight forwarder rates are at least as low as LCL and LTL rates. On longer hauls, they can be significantly lower (NIGP, 2000).

Air freight forwarders operate in a manner similar to the truck and rail industries. Many companies offer a combination of surface and air transport for their shipments, which can result in a great deal of flexibility to their clients. Air freight forwarders can use their ground transportation carriers to offset the overall shipping costs, making it less expensive than direct air service.

Brokers

Freight brokers are similar to forwarders in that they can provide transportation to firms with LCL and LTL shipping needs. The broker is actually an individual or firm that acts as an intermediary between a buyer and a seller (Hinkelman, 2000). They are experts within the transportation industry and usually very well connected. They broker the shipments and coordinate the transportation with one or more carriers, making sure that the goods end up at the right place at the right time. Serving as an agent to both parties (buyer and seller), the broker normally works on a commission basis. Sometimes the term "broker" may not be viewed favorably within the public sector, as it is not actually the firm "doing the work." However, in the logistics arena, brokers can provide a valuable service to the government, offering a level of shipping expertise that can benefit the organization on an as-needed basis as well as saving the agency transportation costs.

Designing a Transportation Program

Historically, the public sector has left the transportation decision to the supplier. However, some agencies are seeing the benefits of taking more control of freight movements. Pinkerton and Marien (1997) offer some important guidelines for establishing a good transportation program. Once it is determined that purchasing and supply will control inbound transportation, efforts should be coordinated with the supplier. Initially, suppliers may be resistant to this change in business practices, and it is important to obtain their cooperation. Additionally, they may offer important contacts in the transportation industry that will be needed to coordinate freight movements from their facility to the final destination.

A team effort is...

important to assure

success, no mat-

ter the size of the

agency.

A team effort is also important to assure success, no matter the size of the agency. Key members of the team should include transportation/traffic, operations, inventory management, warehousing, supply quality assurance, and accounting—with purchasing and supply management taking the lead.

Carrier Selection Checklist

There are many things to consider when selecting a transportation carrier. Using the **right** carrier to deliver the needed goods at the **right** location continues to be an extremely important theory. The condition of the goods and the timing of delivery are a direct reflection on the procurement department. The following list represents some key areas to consider during carrier selection.

- What types of goods will be moved?
- What is the best mode of transportation? Are multiple modes required?
- What are the agencies shipping points and "traffic lanes" with the highest volumes?
- What are the delivery requirements?
- What is the best method of solicitation (IFB, RFP, negotiation, etc.)?
- What criteria will be used for selection? (cost, financial stability, past performance, service capacity, etc.)?
- Who owns the goods during transit, and who is responsible for claims?
- What are the standards of operation for the contractor?
- How are billings and payments handled?
- Will assignment of the agreement to another party be allowed?
- Is the contract renewable for additional terms?
- How are acts of God (force majeure) dealt with, such as weather delays?
- What constitutes a contract breach, and what is the result?
- What are the remedies for disputes between the parties?

This list offers some important areas to consider for procurement professionals responsible for transportation services; however, it is certainly not all-inclusive. Much discussion and collaboration with using departments should occur when selecting a carrier to fill an organization's transportation needs. Additionally, it may be necessary to outsource some of the transportation functions to a third party, particularly if staffing is limited. Third-party logistics providers still allow purchasing and supply control of the transportation decision, but offer their expertise and a variety of options and services.

Delivery Terms

There are numerous types of shipping terms, with each term identifying certain rights and responsibilities of both the buyer and seller. Issues like carrier selection, routing, and the transfer of title are all a part of these terms. The subject of ownership is important, particularly if the goods are lost or damaged in transit. Whichever party owns the goods, in accordance with the freight terms, is responsible for filing any damage claims.

The term F.O.B. stands for "free on board," indicating that the price for freight includes delivery at the seller's expense to some specified point. The terms *destination* and *point of origin* describe a specific point and the responsibilities of buyer and seller. Point of origin means that the title and control are transferred to the buyer, along with any risks of transportation, once the carrier signs the bill of lading. The buyer must also file any claims for loss or damage. However, routing of the shipment is at the discretion of the buyer. Destination indicates that the seller owns and controls the freight until it is delivered to the buyer and the contract for carriage is concluded. The seller takes responsibility for selecting the carrier and assumes all responsibility for any risks of transportation. The seller also files any claims for loss or damage. Several terms are used to describe payment terms. Table 3 provides a summary of shipping options.

Freight Terms	Customer Takes Title of Goods	Customer Responsibilities	Supplier Responsibilities
F.O.B. Point of Origin, Freight Collect	At point of origin or factory	Pays freight, bears freight charges,* owns goods in transit, files claims for loss or damage	
F.O.B. Point of Origin, Freight Prepaid and Allowed	At point of origin or factory	Owns goods in transit, files claims	Pays freight, bears freight charges*
F.O.B. Point of Origin, Freight Prepaid and Added	At point of origin or factory	Bears freight charges, owns goods in transit, files claims	Pays freight, adds freight to invoice
F.O.B. Destination, Freight Collect	At destination	Pays freight, bears freight charges	Owns goods in transit, files claims
F.O.B. Destination, Freight Prepaid and Added	At destination	Bears freight charges	Pays freight, adds freight to invoice, owns goods in transit, files claims
F.O.B. Destination, Freight Prepaid and Allowed	At destination		Pays freight, bears freight charges,* owns goods in transit, files claims

*The party who bears the freight charges is responsible for payment made to the carrier and is liable for nonpayment; payment of charges by a party does not necessarily indicate responsibility.

Table 3. *F.O.B. Shipping Terms*

Source: National Institute of Governmental Purchasing, Inc. (NIGP) (2004). *Sourcing in the Public Sector.* Herndon, VA: NIGP.

The most common delivery term has been the requirement for *F.O.B. Destination, Freight Prepaid and Allowed* within the public agency's bidding documents. In such instances, the selected vendor handles all aspects of product delivery, with the agency taking ownership upon delivery (Stanley & Matthews, 2002). In situations where the F.O.B. term is silent, or not addressed in the contract, then *F.O.B. Origin* applies as far as the passage of title in accordance with the Uniform Commercial Code (UCC).

If an organization chooses to manage the transportation function, another option is *F.O.B. Point of Origin*, with the option of *Freight Collect* or *Freight Prepaid and Added*. These terms should be used when it can be determined that there will be cost savings because actual freight charges are less than those built into the cost of goods purchased. Sometimes, having the purchasing organization make arrangements for the shipment of large and bulky items requiring use of an entire freight car or a full truck could result in significant savings. Examples include rolls of paper for large print jobs or road salt during the winter. An organization may also wish to deal exclusively with one carrier for all of its shipping needs. Possessing a good working knowledge of the delivery terms and knowing how to apply them appropriately when dealing with carriers can lead to an overall reduction in an organization's freight costs (Mankin, 1997).

Understanding Tariffs

Tariffs are published schedules of a carrier's rates. The transportation industry is particularly competitive today, not only within a particular mode but between modes. It is important to understand the rate structure offered by each carrier for each mode. Today, tariffs are often provided on a carrier's Web site. Carriers frequently offer more than one rate tariff as well as a rules tariff and a liability tariff.

Tracing Shipments

It may be necessary to locate a shipment that is in transit and still under the control of the carrier. Today, most tracking systems are automated and available online using satellite technology. Information that may be needed to track a shipment includes (a) shipment origin, (b) destination, (c) date shipped, (d) freight bill number, and (e) description of goods.

Freight Invoices

A freight bill should never be paid until it has been audited. If in-house staff is not available to review bills, preferably before they are paid, special auditing firms are available that charge a commission on any savings from overcharges. Organizations have up to six months to audit freight bills. Overcharging may occur for a number of reasons, including (a) incorrect classification, (b) rate calculation mistakes, (c) incorrect F.O.B. terms, (d) incorrect routing, (e) poor delivery, (f) incorrect packaging, and (g) miscellaneous additional charges that are not justifiable.

Carrier Performance

The carrier's performance should be reviewed periodically and used to improve performance of the organization. Carriers may provide their own report card with information on shipment and delivery dates. There are multiple measures that can be applied, including (a) billing accuracy, (b) frequency of claims, (c) delivery performance, (d) rate negotiations, (e) technology offered, (f) equipment, and (g) post-evaluation performance.

Conclusion

There are several modes of transportation that are available to the government. While some are more commonly used than others, they all have their niche in the world of transportation. Whether it is through the use of truck freight, air shipment, water, railway, or pipelines the public sector must have its goods transferred. Each type of transportation mode has its own set of advantages and disadvantages. While motor carriage is extremely flexible and affordable, after examining all costs and factors involved, the best decision in a given situation may be to use next-day air transport. Procurement professionals can make the right decisions for their agencies only by knowing all of the options available and the nuances of each. There should be many considerations when selecting a carrier. Securing a company that is dependable and accountable can prove to be invaluable. Careful attention should be given to the procurement method employed as well as the carrier selection itself.

Contracting for auxiliary services can be a valuable venture for the government. Third-party logistics providers that can perform functions, such as warehousing and distribution, can assist small and large agencies alike. It may be time to consider outside expertise to supplement the public workforce, particularly with today's shrinking budgets. Even if shipping services are needed on an infrequent basis, using service providers such as freight forwarders and brokers can make a lot of sense. Research supports the fact that more and more areas are being considered for outsourcing, so it is time to stay current on which tasks may prove beneficial from outsourcing possibilities. Whenever public policy dictates the use of such third-party providers, the procurement professional will be the leader in integrating these services into agency operations.

The area of transportation may have been historically overlooked and under-valued, but it has truly evolved into a critical component of government procurement. While the purchase of the right goods and materials is crucial, so is ensuring that those goods arrive at their proper destination when they are needed. Transportation has played a significant role in the economic development of the United States and continues to be a key element of our National economy. As procurement professionals interact with these transportation carriers, they also become a part of this important industry. What does the future hold? Most experts feel that changes will occur but that transportation will remain a strong and specialized field. With the expected turnover of motor carriers, consolidation of express mail firms, and increased use of eCommerce, procurement professionals will need to adapt in order to remain successful in the public sector.

References

Bohman, R. (2002, August). Who's responsible for loading or unloading the freight? *Logistics Management*.

Coyle, J. J., Bardi, E. J., & Langley, C. J., Jr. (1996). *The management of business logistics*. St. Paul, MN: West Publishing Company.

DeWitt, D., & Clinger, J. (2000). *Intermodal freight transportation*. Millennium Paper, TRB Committee on Intermodal Freight Transportation. Washington, DC: National Academy Press.

Duffy, R. J. (1999, March). Logistics: A custom link. *Purchasing Today, 10*(3).

Ernst & Young. (1999). *Third-party logistics: Views from the customers.* Ernst & Young, Fourth Annual Study. Knoxville: University of Tennessee.

Hinkelman, E. G. (2000). *Dictionary of international trade* (4th ed.). Novato, CA: World Trade Press.

Konezny G. P., & Beskow, M. J. (1999). *Third party logistics: Improving global supply chain performance*. Minneapolis, MN: Piper Jaffray Equity Research.

Kuglin, F. A. (1998). *Customer centered supply chain management*. New York: AMACOM, American Management Association.

Leenders, M. R., & Flynn, A. E. (1995). *Value-driven purchasing*. New York: National Association of Purchasing Management and Irwin Professional Publishing.

Mankin, R. T. (1997, July). Understanding the ins and outs of carrier terms. *Purchasing Today*, 36.

McGinnis, M. A. (1990, Fall). The relative importance of cost and service in freight transportation choice: Before and after deregulation. *Transportation Journal*, 12-19.

National Association of State Procurement Officials (NASPO). (2001). *State and local government purchasing principles and practices*. Lexington, KY: NASPO.

National Institute of Governmental Purchasing, Inc. (NIGP) (2004). *Sourcing in the Public Sector*. Herndon, VA: NIGP.

Pinkerton, R. L., & Marien, E. J. (1997, April). The fundamentals of inbound transportation. *NAPM InfoEdge, 2*(8).

Stanley, L. L., & Matthews, D. L. (in press). Logistics and transportation. *Encyclopedia of Public Administration and Public Policy*. New York: Dekker Encyclopedias, Taylor and Francis Books.

WEFA-DRI. (2001a). *Air transportation industry yearbook 2001/2002*. New York: WEFA-DRI.

WEFA-DRI. (2001b). *Railroad transportation industry yearbook 2001/2002*. New York: WEFA-DRI.

WEFA-DRI. (2001c). *Truck transportation industry yearbook 2001/2002*. New York: WEFA-DRI.

WEFA-DRI. (2001d). *Water transportation industry yearbook 2001/2002*. New York: WEFA-DRI.

Wood, D. F., & Johnson, J. C. (1995) *Contemporary transportation* (5th ed.). Upper Saddle River, NJ: Prentice Hall.

Chapter 4

Costs Of Transportation

Basic Transportation Costs

From an economics standpoint, there are four basic costs of transportation. ***Fixed costs*** are those costs that do not change when there is a change in output—and remain constant regardless of the level of activity. For example, airlines make a significant investment in airplanes; motor carriers own a fleet of trucks; and railroads purchase railroad cars and terminals. Pipelines and railroads are classified as fixed-cost modes because of significant investments in their path of travel.

Variable costs are those costs which change as the level of output changes. Fuel costs, wages and maintenance costs are all examples of variable costs. All costs eventually become variable since items considered to be fixed assets will have to be replaced. Northwest Airlines is currently in the process of retiring their Boeing 747s and replacing them with newer, more fuel-efficient equipment. Airlines, water carriers and motor carriers incur a large proportion of variable costs, such as fuel, maintenance, and labor, simply because they do not own their travel path. Cities own the airports and ports, requiring airlines and water carriers to pay user fees—another variable cost (Bloomberg, LeMay, & Hanna, 2001).

Joint costs occur when a cost will result in the production of more than one product. For example, if Burlington Northern provides rail movement from Kansas City to Houston, there might be the possibility of back-haul service or additional service to another destination, say Brownsville, Texas. This means that the cost that was originally considered to directly apply to the trip from Kansas City to Houston could now also apply to another trip, such as the backhaul from Houston to Brownsville. Variable and fixed costs can also be joint costs. All modes of transportation incur joint costs to some extent.

Common costs are shared costs that cannot be directly associated with a particular activity or activities. These costs are encountered by all modes of transportation. For example, ABC Trucking, a hypothetical trucking firm, is moving goods from Portland to Sacramento. The truck contains five separate shipments and breaks down in transit. How should the cost of repairs be allocated? Repairs would be a common cost in that they would have to be shared by all of those using the truck. These costs could be compared to overhead costs. Would they be shared by weight, cubic space, or both?

Relationship between Demand and Transportation Costs

Transportation carriers must consider other factors when pricing their services. They must consider the demand of one shipper, known as *disaggregate demand*, versus the demand from all shippers, known as *aggregate demand*. For example, if Union Pacific Railroad has a 100-car rail car movement from Salt Lake City to Denver, each car may be carrying a different commodity with a different origin, a different destination, and different demand characteristics. Some cars may carry coal, others automobiles, and still others containers filled with a mix of products. The cost of one movement of 100 rail cars is the same, but pricing will vary depending on individual demand. The elasticity of demand for different products also affects the rates carriers can charge.

The elasticity of demand related to transportation has three important components. The first is actual demand for the commodity or final product. If the demand for this item is *elastic*, or sensitive to price changes, then demand for the transportation of this item will also be elastic. The elasticity of demand for transportation is frequently dependent upon the ratio of transportation charges to the final product price. However, demand for the same commodity may vary from city to city. For example, companies located in Austin may be willing to pay $2.73 for a bushel of wheat, while companies located in Denver may be willing to pay $2.90 per bushel. Therefore, a middleman should be willing to pay up to $.17 per bushel to move the wheat to Denver. This is known as the spread in price between two locations.

Secondly, if demand for a product/commodity is *inelastic*, i.e., demand is not sensitive to price changes or demand is somewhat fixed in quantity, then transportation charges are considered an input to the inelasticity of demand. Thus, demand for the transportation mode is also considered inelastic. For example, the demand for petroleum products is considered inelastic; therefore, demand for tanker ships is also considered inelastic.

A third element is the *time elasticity* of transportation. An investment in purchased products includes opportunity costs incurred while in transit. The product is not available for use until it is received and money has been allocated for the purchase through a purchase order that can not be used for any other purposes. At times, shippers are willing to pay more to reduce freight time and gain access to that product more quickly, e.g., by using air versus truck or rail. Perishable products such as food for cafeterias are particularly sensitive to transit times.

Shippers lose potential sales if food is less than fresh upon arrival as a result of longer transit time and, therefore, are willing to pay more in transportation costs.

Basis for Determining Transportation Rates

Theoretically, carriers examine two factors to establish their rates, as shown in Figure 5: (a) the actual cost of providing their service(s), or *cost of service*, and (b) the value of their services to the shipper, or *value of service* (Coyle, Bardi, & Langley, (1996). The cost-of-service approach takes a supply side view and sets the "floor" or baseline for rates. Ideally, a particular rate would cover the fixed and variable costs of providing movement of those goods plus some additional margin for profit (Lambert, Stock, & Ellram, 1998). However, in some instances, a carrier might simply try to recover its *marginal*, or out-of-pocket expenses. What are some of these expenses? How are they different from other costs identified, such as joint cost and direct costs? At the upper end, a carrier would attempt to recover the full cost of providing the service. Somewhere in between, carriers may charge an average of their variable or total costs.

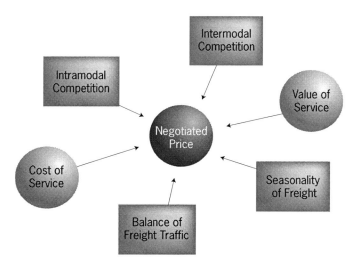

Figure 5. *Factors affecting rates.*

The difficulty in this approach lies in accurately identifying the fixed and variable costs and then determining a method of allocating a portion of their fixed costs to each shipment. Carriers incur common and joint costs when they consolidate shipments of two or more shippers into one movement, thus making it more difficult to determine fixed and variable costs. In practice, determining the cost of service is frequently used for low-value products with thin profit margins. Carriers make use of cross-subsidies, charging rates based on marginal rates for one product and higher rates on other products, to recoup the total costs.

Carriers also may charge based on the *value of service* provided, or what the traffic will allow. This method goes back to the demand side of pricing; thus, rates will vary by product. Factors affecting rates include: (a) amount of competition within a mode; (b) amount of competition between modes; (c) balance of freight traffic in and out of a market; and (d) seasonality of a product movement.

Other variables are factored into the rate equation as well. The distance of a movement is one variable. Longer hauls generally result in higher transportation rates but are not always proportional. Carriers may also offer blanket rates that cover all points within a geographical area.

Carriers also factor in the weight of the movement. Rates are quoted in cents per hundredweight (cwt), which is determined by dividing the actual weight in pounds by 100. Additionally, carriers offer discounts for shipping in large quantities. For example, railroads will charge less per cwt for shipping full carloads (CL) versus less than carload (LCL). Similarly, motor carriers will charge less per cwt if a shipper is moving full truckloads (TL) rather than less-than-truckloads (LTL). The cost differential can be attributed to additional time and labor involved in consolidating multiple shipments because of additional stops and more frequent unloading.

As dollar values increase, transportation costs tend to increase because there is a greater chance of damage... resulting in higher insurance costs.

The dollar value of the product will influence rates charged. As dollar values increase, transportation costs tend to increase because there is a greater chance of damage, i.e., a greater risk in moving higher dollar items, resulting in higher insurance costs. The transportation company will have to pay more to reimburse the shipper should damage occur.

The density of a product, or weight/space ratio, can impact carrier rates. The greater the density, the lower the transportation costs. For example, the movement of boxed furniture, considered to have a high density, would result in lower rates than non-stackable baskets.

Carriers must factor in the risk of damage to a product. The greater chance of damage, such as in the case of breakables or oddly shaped items, the higher the transportation costs.

Special handling is another consideration. Products requiring refrigeration, heating, or special stops during transit would result in higher transportation costs.

Stow ability, or cube utilization, is the degree to which a product fills available space within a boxcar, trailer, container, etc. Easier stow ability results in lower rates. Petroleum products, for example, are easily stowed, while autos or machinery are not.

Finally, the extent of government regulation will have an impact on rates. Factors such as safety requirements, regulations on the movement of hazardous materials and labor laws, to mention a few, all add costs to transportation movements and are factored into the rates charged.

Specific Pricing Issues

An examination of some of the basics of transportation costs and pricing leads to the various ways that carriers charge for services. Understanding the types of pricing structures prevalent in the marketplace is essential to properly applying them to a particular purchase or acquisition for an organization.

Class Rates

The first step in the rate-making process is classification of commodities. There are over 33,000 major shipping and receiving points in the United States alone (Coyle et al., 1996). There are also thousands of possible products and commodities that can be shipped. Since it is not feasible to establish a separate rate for every good that is transported, the National Classification Committee (NCC) combines commodities together in common categories or *classes*. The NCC, established in 1956 by the Interstate Commerce Commission (ICC), is the primary classification body within the motor carrier industry. The NCC is still in existence today, operating under the auspices of the Surface Transportation Board (STB). Each class has an assigned number, which increases as transportation of the commodity becomes more difficult. Motor carriers use this classification system to apply a rate to the specific class. The *rate basis* is a formula of specific factors or elements that control the setting of a rate. A rate can be based on any number of factors, i.e., weight, measure, equipment type, package and/or box size.

Currently, rates may be set by the carrier or collectively by a motor rate bureau, but most carriers set their own rates. Regional motor rate bureaus, however, have developed nationwide rating systems that can be used by shippers as a starting point for negotiation of rates (Bohman, 2001). For example, CzarLite™ was created by SMC3 (Southern Motor Carriers Rate Conference) and provides benchmark rates without adjustments made by individual carriers.

Commodity Rates

Approximately 90% of CL or TL shipments move under commodity or exception rates. (Materials shipped under commodity rates are always in CL or TL lots.) A commodity rate is a unique, published rate established for the shipment of a particular good transported by rail or truck in large quantities between set locations and is separate from the classification system. Commodity rates are generally much less expensive than class rates (National Institute of Governmental Purchasing, Inc. [NIGP], 2000). Motor carriers have also created commodity rates using zip codes to determine origin and destination points.

Exception Rates

Carriers will publish exception rates that allow for different transportation characteristics for a commodity based on significant competition from other carriers or larger volume movements within a geographical area. An exception rate supersedes any previously published classification rate. However, there are other special rates designed to meet particular situations and are briefly described below.

Freight All Kinds (FAK). Also known as all-commodity rates, carriers quote a rate in dollars per hundredweight or total dollars per shipment. Shipments are generally a mixed assortment of various types of freight going to one destination, and the cost to ship is the primary consideration rather than the freight's value.

Value Rates. Value rates are generally applicable in the movement of household goods. The liability to the carrier, based on the value of the freight, is the basis for the rate charged. A fixed amount of liability is determined, usually set at cents per pound.

Deferred Rates. Carriers may offer lower rates if the shipper is willing to accept a later arrival time. This rate allows the carrier greater flexibility in loading and moving the freight. The United Parcel Service, Federal Express, and the U.S. Postal Service are examples of organizations offering deferred rates.

Multiple-Vehicle Rates. Railroads may offer discounts to purchase transportation for multiple carloads of a particular commodity by offering multiple-vehicle rates. Lower transportation costs improve the railroads' economies of scale and make them more competitive with motor carriers. The *unit train rate* is an extension of multiple-vehicle rates, in which a rate is quoted for an entire train carrying one commodity.

Incentive Rates. A carrier may offer published incentive rates to encourage shippers to move larger loads, resulting in better utilization of equipment. The shipper pays a flat rate for freight up to a certain weight and then a lower rate for any freight above that weight.

Negotiated Rates. Carriers are frequently willing to negotiate rates. Consider the case of a shipper moving truckloads of freight on a regular basis; they could negotiate a lower rate. Additionally, discounts may be negotiated on LTL rates.

Joint Rates. A joint rate is used for hauling a single shipment over two or more independent transportation lines, which cooperate to offer a "through service." The shipment travels on one bill of lading.

Tapered Rates. Carriers' rates may increase but not directly proportional to the increase in distance. Tapered rates result when carriers are able to spread their fixed shipment costs over a greater number of miles traveled. A trucking firm may charge a rate of $4.00 to move freight 100 miles and $6.00 to move that same freight 200 miles. While the distance increased by 100%, the rate increase was only 50%.

Stated Rates. A stated rate may be established for direct routes from one point to another. Rates via other routes between the same points are set in relation to the standard rate.

Through Rates. Through rates are applicable for transportation from point of origin to destination, including any stops-in-transit. However, a stop-off charge will be assessed for any intermediate stops. A through rate may be either a joint rate or a combination of two or more rates.

Differential Rates. A differential rate is the amount added to or subtracted from a through rate to establish a rate. For example, the rate from Chicago to Philadelphia is made up of the basis rate (Chicago to New York) less the differential basis (or rate) to Philadelphia.

Ocean Freight Rates. Ocean freight rates are typically quoted based on *weight-ton* or *measurement-ton*. A weight-ton varies and is classified as (a) *short*, equal to 2000 pounds; (b) *long*, equal to 2,240 pounds, or (c) *metric*, equal to 2,205 pounds. A measurement-ton is equal to 40 cubic feet. Carriers may also quote based on container rates. In addition, charges may be added to the cost of the shipment, which could include terminal handling fees, fuel adjustment factors, and adjustments for current rates.

Alternative Transportation Services

Charges for services other than basic transportation may be incurred and will appear in the contract for service. Canadian National Railroad (CN), for example, will charge for the following services (www.cn.ca):

- Automotive compound services
- Diversion
- Inspection services
- Loading/unloading
- Product transfer
- Special train assignment
- Storage
- Intermodal terminal services
- Trucking
- Car cleaning
- Equipment use/rental
- Labor
- Out-of-line haul
- Protective services
- Stop-off
- Switching
- CargoFlo™ terminal services
- Weighing

Other fees are also charged as penalties, including:

- Demurrage
- Missing/late documentation
- Intermodal container detention
- Overloads

Terminal Services

Carriers own terminals where a number of functions may be performed, which affect the length of transit time. For example, *dunnage,* material used to protect or support freight in or on rail cars and trucks, may be required. Bracing, false floors, and racks are common forms of dunnage. A specified amount of dunnage often can be used to transport a shipment without charging for the dunnage, but it is important to check the appropriate published tariff.

Smaller LTL shipments may be *consolidated* or *concentrated* at the terminal into one or more large shipments to keep costs down. Shipments also arrive at the terminal for dispersion— the breaking down of a consolidated shipment into smaller shipments for individual consignees.

The carrier is obligated to load and unload LTL and LCL shipments. TL and CL shipments must be loaded by the shipper, but the consignee must unload, although the carrier is often willing to perform this function at an additional cost. Typically, a carrier will designate a certain amount of time for loading and unloading the vehicle. However, charges are assessed for vehicles detained beyond that point. *Demurrage* is the term used for storage charges assessed by railroads for rail cars, while *detention* applies to excessive storage of trucks or containers.

Consolidation and *dispersion* involve other *shipment service* functions, including billing, routing and other clerical duties. The carrier must also maintain an adequate number of vehicles to meet shipping demands. Freight may be transferred at the terminal from one vehicle to another to provide through service.

Carriers also monitor shipments to assure they were properly weighed and reach their intended destination. Carriers maintain proper weighing equipment and may be asked to re-weigh a shipment should the shipper feel the original weight recorded was incorrect. *Tracing* is another common practice in the industry to determine the exact location of a shipment anytime during transit. Today, carriers offer shippers instant tracing through their Internet sites. A carrier may be required to *expedite* a shipment by tracing it and then finding a way to decrease transit time. Shipments are sometimes miscarried or unloaded at the wrong terminal, which is called *free astray*. Free astray shipments are billed and forwarded to the correct terminal free of charge to the shipper.

Line-Haul Services

Line-haul services include additional services for the shipper while goods are in transit. *Diversion* and *reconsignment* are terms used interchangeably to describe a change in the shipment's consignee, consignor, routing, and/or original destination. However, diversion specifically applies to those changes in destination or routing before arrival of the shipment at the original destination, while reconsignment refers to changes in consignee before or after arrival of the shipment at the original destination (www.csx.com). Shippers of perishable products commonly use this service. Shippers also have an option known as *transit privilege*, which allows them to store a shipment while in transit or to make changes that physically alter the shipment. For example, a shipper might stop a lumber shipment for additional processing before it continues on to its final destination.

Shippers may choose to stop a shipment during transit to allow for loading or partial unloading, known as *stopping in transit*. The shipper pays charges based on the highest shipment weight at any time during transit. *Stop-off charges* are assessed for each intermediate stop.

> *Line-haul services include additional services for the shipper while goods are in transit.*

A shipper may want to *pool* several LCL or LTL shipments into CL and TL shipments bound for one destination and one consignee. Carriers typically make the delivery to a warehouse or independently owned *drayage company*, which then breaks down the shipment and makes deliveries to individual consignees. Carriers often assign *pool cars* (rail) or *pool trucks* for specific industries, commodities, or locations. The total cost for this service is less than if the shipment was not originally pooled because the shipper is charged CL or TL rates.

Total Logistics Costs Concepts

The previous discussion strictly focused on the costs and pricing of transportation. The goal of most shippers, in fact, is to minimize charges by the carrier. However, the decision should involve not only the costs of transportation but also other logistics costs, such as inventory holding costs and packaging costs, with the desired result being "overall" lower logistics expenditures. Known as a *systems approach*, the importance of each logistical function is recognized, but the interdependence of the various functions are also acknowledged. Thus, we recognize that there will be cost tradeoffs. Some of these logistical functions may include:

- Customer service (internal & external)
- Documentation flows
- Order management and processing
- Warehouse site selection
- Recycling and disposal
- Warehouse management (Wood & Johnson, 1995).
- Demand forecasting
- Inventory management
- Packaging
- Supply management
- Transportation management

Imagine that a county in Texas might be able to reduce its overall logistics costs by consolidating several warehouses into one. This consolidation may result in higher transportation costs, but the offset still results in overall lower logistics costs. Similarly, a county in Oregon may determine that shipping purchased goods by truck rather than rail results in higher transportation costs, but inventory-carrying costs are reduced significantly because less inventory is required to meet internal user requirements.

To implement a total logistics cost approach, there are two means of analysis.

One method is *short-run,* or *static analysis* (Coyle et al., 1996). Using this method, data is reviewed and compared at one point in time. Cost information is developed for each alternative, and a system is selected based on overall lowest costs.

Example of Short-Run (Static) Analysis

The City of Winter Lake Park currently purchases mulch for several parks. The supplier delivers 60,000 cubic yards of mulch by rail to the City's centralized warehouse where the mulch is bagged and then delivered by truck to each park. The City is considering a second alternative. The supplier would ship the mulch directly to each park by truck. To keep costs down, the total amount of mulch needed would be shipped at one time but would make deliveries to each park. The trade-off in this instance would be somewhat higher transportation costs of trucking versus the additional storage at the centralized warehouse and labor costs to bag and deliver the mulch to each park. A non-cost factor that the City might consider is customer service—Will the mulch be delivered more quickly and at the right time with the proposed system?

The second method is *long-run* or *dynamic analysis.* Break-even analysis is used to determine which of two or more logistics systems results in lower overall costs at a given volume of shipments. Fixed and variable costs are taken into consideration to evaluate the total cost for each alternative. However, the difficulty with break-even analysis is usually attributed to assigning costs to the fixed or variable category.

Example of Long-Run (Dynamic) Analysis

The City of Winter Lake Park is also interested in determining which alternative will be less expensive in the future, given that the City will be building two new parks in the next two years and demand for mulch will increase. Under the current method of operation (Alternative 1) the City has fixed costs of $6,000 and pays $0.042 per bag in variable costs to deliver the mulch. Under the proposed system (Alternative 2), the City would pay lower fixed costs ($5,800) but higher variable costs ($0.055) to deliver the mulch.

To calculate the breakeven point, the problem can be set up as follows:

Current Method = **Alternative 1**
Total cost = fixed cost + variable cost/unit * number of units
= $6,000 + $0.042x

Proposed Method = **Alternative 2**
Total cost = $5,800 + $0.055x

Trade-off point
$6000 + $0.042x = $5,800 + $0.055x
$0.11x = $200 = .013x
x = 15,385 cubic yards

Thus, if the City orders 15,385 cubic yards of mulch, it is indifferent as to whether it uses the first or second alternative. If the City's demand is less than 15,385 cubic yards, it will be more cost effective to use the current system; if demand exceeds the breakeven point, the proposed system will be less expensive. Thus, with construction of new parks, the City may want to rethink its current system and adopt the second alternative once the demand for mulch exceeds 15,385 cubic yards. In this particular case, when the volume is less than 15,385, the second option is a better solution. When the volume is greater than 15,385, the first option is more economical. To prove this point, the total costs for each alternative can be computed for a demand of 60,000 cubic yards:

Alternative 1
Total cost = $6,000 + $0.042 (60,000) = $8520

Alternative 2
Total cost = $5,800 + $0.055 (60,000) = $9100

The break-even point can also be shown in the form of a graph (Figure 6).

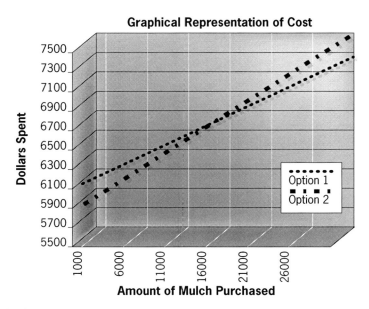

Figure 6. *Graph of break-even point.*

Conclusion

There are a number of factors that can impact the rate that a shipper is charged for transporting materials. Whether it is based upon the type of goods being shipped, the distance they are traveling, or the number of containers used, a rate needs to be established so that all parties involved understand the cost of moving the materials from origin to destination. Professionals working within transportation and logistics should be familiar with the terminology of the shipping world in order to interact with shippers and third-party providers in the best way.

References

Bloomberg, D. J., LeMay, S., & Hanna, J. B. (2002). *Logistics.* Upper Saddle River, NJ: Prentice Hall.

Bohman, R. (2001, August 1). CzarLite and MARS: Two LTL pricing initiatives. *Logistics Management.*

Coyle, J. J., Bardi, E. J., & Langley, C. J., Jr. (1996). *The management of business logistics* (6th ed.). Minneapolis/St. Paul, MN: West Publishing Company.

Lambert, D. M., Stock, J. R., & Ellram, L. M. (1998). *Fundamentals of logistics management.* Boston: Irwin McGraw-Hill.

National Institute of Governmental Purchasing, Inc. (NIGP) (2000). *Intermediate public procurement* (2nd ed.). Herndon, VA: NIGP.

Wood, D. F., & Johnson, J. C. (1995) *Contemporary transportation* (5th ed.). Upper Saddle River, NJ: Prentice Hall.

Chapter 5

The Transportation Contract

Asound contract can provide many advantages for a public agency. Formal, written agreements that secure pricing, minimize risk, and protect an organization's interests are essential. These concepts also apply to transportation contracts. Similar to other buying agreements, the procurement professional is responsible for the transportation contract. From vendor sourcing, to the solicitation process, to contract award, and even through administration, the public procurement professional makes sure that everything comes together as planned. Transportation contracts should be viewed much like any other type of public contract. A report published by the Center for Advanced Purchasing Studies (CAPS) revealed that over 50% of U.S. procurement departments are responsible for inbound transportation services (Gentry, 1991).

Negotiation and Transportation

Depending on the organization involved, the ability to negotiate may be limited. Many state and local agencies can negotiate contracts, while others may have rules that prohibit negotiation on certain contract types. Historically, government agencies have negotiated services for engineering, consulting, and information technology; but, today many entities are using the Request for Proposal (RFP) process to select other key service providers. A survey by the National Association of State Procurement Officials (NASPO) found that 93% of the agencies surveyed used RFPs to select services (NASPO, 2002). Regardless of an individual organization's rules, there are concepts and strategies that will be useful in the contracting process.

According to the National Institute of Governmental Purchasing, Inc. (NIGP) (2002), "negotiate" is "to communicate or confer with another to reach an agreement or compromise to settle some matter." Within this framework, all public agencies would seemingly perform some type of negotiation. Whether it is during the contract award process, in the midst of a direct negotiation, haggling over change orders, or resolving contractor disputes, the procurement professional appears to be heavily involved in this arena. Negotiation is a part of the day-to-day work environment in government. Work processes, including staffing resources, policy decisions, and budget appropriations all require negotiation. Negotiation skills, therefore, become just as valuable internally as they are externally.

Carrier selection and the possible selection methods are decisions that need to be made. Transportation services can be either dealt with in a separate contract or incorporated into the agreement for the goods purchased. The latter appears to be the most common approach in government. Whichever method is chosen, it is important that an organization address the transportation issue and ensure that a contract is in place to cover the service. As is the case with other contracts, specific contract terms that have been negotiated can prove to be invaluable, often "saving the day" for the organization.

Keys to Successful Negotiation

According to Leenders and Flynn (1995), the key to any successful negotiation is proper planning. This means that considerable thought and time should be devoted to the negotiation effort. Very likely, the other party has spent time preparing for the negotiation so that their interests are protected. In a contract situation, the procurement professional must be very clear about the objectives of the organization. Is securing the lowest costs the main priority, or is it obtaining the highest level of service for the budgeted amount? Many of today's most successful negotiators prepare by developing a written negotiation plan. This document can include background information, key strategic issues, organizational objectives, cost parameters, and agency concessions. A thorough plan can be very advantageous in assisting the procurement professionals to prepare for negotiations and can help to steer the focus toward key issues while keeping agency staff on track and the negotiation team on target.

...the key to any successful negotiation is proper planning.

The following is an eight-step plan for carrying out negotiations. Each of these steps is important and, when executed together, can help ensure a successful negotiation.

Basic Groundwork. The first step is preparation, which includes understanding the facts of the situation, evaluating options and alternatives, and setting objectives. Suppliers may provide useful information on past experiences with carriers. Carriers will also need to know about the organization, the products to be shipped, shipping destinations, special handling requirements, and service expectations. According to Stroh (2002), some important facts to gather include:

- Class ratings for all products (for trucking and rail);
- Freight tonnage;
- Amount previously spent on transportation services;
- Frequency of shipments;
- Freight payment record; and
- Expected delivery times and windows.

Developing Objectives for the Negotiation Plan. In order to prepare a negotiation plan, specific objectives and strategies must be developed. This includes selecting the negotiation team, tactics, and site.

Gaining Support. Prior to the start of the negotiations, the negotiation team must have full management support and the negotiation plan must be consistent with organizational objectives.

Team Work. The team leader (i.e., lead negotiator) should convene a meeting with all of the members to discuss goals and strategies and to review strengths and weaknesses. The role that each member will play, including the lead negotiator, should be well defined.

Live Action. This step includes the negotiation process itself, which should take place preferably face-to-face with the other party. Presentation, exploration, and hard bargaining are each a part of the live action.

Verbal Agreement. Once both parties feel that they have reached agreement, the lead negotiator will ensure that key objectives have been met. Any uncertainties should be addressed before reaching verbal agreement.

Written Agreement. The written agreement will confirm and formalize the verbal agreement and will likely involve each party's legal counsel.

Making it Work. Complying with the terms of the agreement and making it work, for both parties, is the real test of its success. This is a good time to evaluate how well the negotiations went and to identify lessons learned for the next negotiation (Leenders & Flynn, 1995).

Tips on Negotiation

Some people are better negotiators than others. While it may seem that certain individuals are "naturals" when it comes to negotiating, they have likely invested time in training and practical application. Negotiation is an area identified by the Center for Advanced Purchasing Studies (CAPS) as a key attribute of world-class purchasers (Duffy, 1999).

Procurement professionals in the public sector need to develop their negotiation skills. The following are some general tips on what makes a good negotiator:

- Knowing that both sides are under pressure so there is no need to be intimidated;
- Wanting to learn new negotiating skills;
- Understanding the art of negotiating;
- Being willing to practice; and
- Wanting to create win/win situations.

Every negotiation is unique. There is a unique set of circumstances and issues surrounding each situation, which must be addressed by the parties involved. There are some common principles that can be applied to just about any situation involving negotiation. The following list can be viewed as some "rules of thumb," as Dawson (1999) identifies several useful tips for negotiators:

- Don't be the first one to name a price.
- Be the one who writes the contract.
- Make offers low but flexible.
- Never be the one to offer to "split the difference."
- Eighty percent of the concessions are made in the last 20 percent of time.
- The person under the greatest time pressure generally loses.
- Never reveal that you have a deadline.
- Avoid negotiating over the phone. (You can't read body language.)
- Watch for sudden changes in body language.

Ability to Negotiate

Within the public sector, there may not be a great deal of negotiation prior to the award of the contract. The crucial terms and conditions should be spelled out in the solicitation document which usually becomes a part of the resulting contract. Many entities include their standard form of contract within the bidding documents so that all offerors can see what the resulting agreement will look like. There may be certain terms that can be negotiated, and these are the points that should be addressed prior to award. Whether the transportation is contracted for separately or as part of the goods acquisition, the seasoned procurement professional will realize the importance of transportation specifics. The data in Table 4 emphasizes the importance of transportation and why careful attention should be paid to this area of the supply chain. Logistics administration and transportation comprise 62% of all domestic supply chain costs.

Supply Chain Area	Total Costs	Percentage
Transportation	$499	58%
Inventory Carrying Costs	$256	30%
Warehousing	$69	8%
Logistics Administration	$38	4%

Table 4. *Components of Domestic Supply Chain ($ in Billions) 1997*

Source: Konezny G. P., & Beskow, M. J. (1999). *Third party logistics: Improving global supply chain performance.* Minneapolis, MN: Piper Jaffray Equity Research.

There are many key considerations when it comes to shipping. Public agencies need to consider these issues when developing solicitations and contracts, acknowledging that every issue is intended to protect the organization's interests and to minimize risk to the greatest extent possible.

Solicitation and Contract Award Considerations

Pricing Implications

A key aspect of any public contract is the pricing. The contract should include the pricing mechanisms used when the services are to be provided. How supplier billings are calculated, and whether they are set rates or discount percentages, need to be addressed in the written agreement. When negotiating with more than one carrier, it is important to use the same rate base consistently. Carriers publish individual rates, but they are often willing to negotiate based on competitors' rates or schedules published by regional rate bureaus. Once a common or "benchmark" rate is established, the purchasing and supply professionals will then be able to make a comparison based on discount levels.

Price may not be the most important element of the contract. If an RFP process is used, service quality and capacity are equally important. If the cost of transportation is included in the purchase of the goods, then the contract should state that all costs and risks associated with the transportation of the goods are to be borne by the supplier. This is the effect of requiring the supplier's pricing to be F.O.B. destination.

Price Changes

While pricing rates may be firm for an initial period of time, costs will likely escalate during the full life of the contract. In virtually all commodity areas, including transportation, prices are subject to change. When such instances do occur, or are proposed by the contractor, there needs to be a common understanding of how this will be handled. It is unrealistic for procurement professionals to expect that the awarded prices will stay firm forever, but there does need to be a clear set of parameters within which prices can change. Perhaps the supplier can propose price increases on an annual basis (i.e., contract anniversary date) as long as the request is substantiated and documented. The rising cost of equipment, fuel, and labor are each likely to play a role. To limit the increase, such factors could be tied to a price index; either a local consumer price index (CPI), a producer price index (PPI), or an industry-specific index. Increases should be formally changed in writing. This function is usually assigned to the procurement professional, who is familiar with the contract and can ensure that any price changes are properly evaluated and processed.

Performance Standards

Today's government purchasers are holding suppliers to a higher standard of performance. As the public sector moves away from transactional-based buying, the need for high-performing suppliers is more important than ever. According to Hutchins (2002), in order to determine world-class performance by a supplier, performance throughout the contract needs to be continuously monitored. Performance metrics need to be agreed upon, including delivery times, allowable material defects, late shipments, material return parameters, and customer response time. These standards should be included in the contract so that they can be accurately measured for compliance.

If a contract calls for the outbound transport of materials, tangible timelines can be set for a response time for pickup requests and delivery time to the final destination. For instance, "carrier shall arrive at owner's dock within four hours of notification" and "contractor agrees to deliver materials shipped from the Salem, Oregon warehouse to the Ontario, Canada plant site within a 24-hour period." The use of "shall" denotes the imperative in contract clauses, while the use of "may" is permissive or optional (NIGP, 2004). It is important that procurement professionals are familiar with these terms and know how and when to use each appropriately. As with any contract, the important areas of performance need to be noted in such a way that they can be monitored during the contract.

Packaging

The proper packaging of goods can protect them from weather and rough handling during transit and ensure that they are in good condition when they reach the buyer's dock.

Many of the goods that are delivered to public agencies are in packaging provided by the manufacturer. Depending on the types of goods being shipped, they may be surrounded by foam peanuts in a cardboard box or strapped to a wooden pallet. Whatever the case, the procurement professional wants to be certain that the goods being purchased are adequately protected while being transported. The packaging material itself may be a small fraction of the cost of the goods but is still an important factor. For example, the microscope being purchased for a police forensics lab is worth thousands of dollars, while the material protecting it is worth just a few dollars. However, that protection may very well save the procurement professional time and money in filing for damages and waiting for a new shipment.

...packaging material itself may be a small fraction of the cost of the goods but is still an important factor.

For larger shipments, there are obviously different packaging requirements. Perhaps potting soil is being purchased for the parks department, and the contract specifies a certain size of bag. Multiple bags are stacked on a pallet, shrink wrapped, and then delivered by the truckload to their destination. Even pallets have varied specifications, including two-way versus four-way entry and returnable versus non-returnable.

The type of packaging that is required should correlate to the available warehouse storage space. If an end-user does not have industrial shelving, it is unlikely that palletized bulk material will do them much good. In those cases, smaller containers and packaging would be specified. Consideration must be given to the cost of carrying large quantities of material, the cost of bulk material versus smaller shipments, and the packaging standards within a given industry. Suppliers may be willing to package goods in whatever way is requested; but, if it is non-standard for them, the price will inevitably increase. One can see that something as seemingly simple as packaging can actually be quite complex.

Consideration should be given as to whether or not the packaging is recyclable. Governments are focusing on sustainability issues in procurement more than ever, with 74% of state governments considering such in the award of the contract (NASPO, 2001). If the packaging material (cardboard, Styrofoam, etc.) can be recycled, it results in less waste going into the landfills.

Reparations

There are occasions when a regulated carrier improperly charges the shipper for transportation aside from loss and damages. Incorrect charges may occur due to duplicate billing, overcharging, or improperly routing a shipment. When refund payments or rebates are made to the shipper to remedy this situation, they are referred to as reparations. The need to file for reparations is discovered during an audit of bills of lading. A complaint is then filed with the Surface Transportation Board, which determines the extent of reparations required. Federal law (U.S. Code, Title 49—Transportation, www.gpoaccess.gov/uscode/browse.html) requires carriers to repay, to the extent possible, all amounts due plus interest.

Overcharges and Undercharges

Overcharges and undercharges are just as their names imply. Based on the correct shipping rate, the amount paid to the carrier is either more or less than is owed. On the government side, the procurement professional is responsible for not overpaying the organization's freight bills. An overpayment can occur when the organization does not pay the freight bill in a timely manner. If the carrier sends a second invoice, the possibility of a double payment for the same shipment of goods may exist.

Most carriers are careful to ensure that they are not undercharging their customers. While the carriers certainly want to collect the full dollar amount owed, they are also legally bound not to undercharge. To charge some customers less than others would constitute discriminatory pricing which is illegal.

Conducting a freight bill audit can determine whether overcharges or undercharges exist, but can also be an added expense to the organization. Such an audit can be handled internally or externally. An internal audit would be conducted by the organization's own employees who would review freight bills and purchase files for discrepancies. If an outside, independent company is used; it is referred to as an external audit. A common arrangement would include an agreement that the independent company would keep a set percentage of any overcharges found. The organization awarding the contract would specify how such an audit would be conducted.

Loss and Damages

Despite each party's best efforts, there is always the possibility of loss or damage during shipment. Loss refers to goods purchased that are missing, as opposed to damaged goods, which actually arrive but are not in an acceptable condition. Normally, whichever party owns the goods during shipment is responsible for the loss or damage. That is a key reason to address the transfer of ownership in the contract or purchase order. The most common term for delivery is *F.O.B. Destination Freight Prepaid and Allowed.*

The proper receipt of goods by the public entity is important. According to Leenders and Flynn 1995), the receiving department generally checks incoming shipments to ensure that (a) the goods were actually ordered by the agency; (b) no visible damage occurred during transit; (c) the quantities received are correct; and (d) the shipping documentation is complete.

The extent of the supplier's obligations should be covered in the agreement in the event of lost or damaged goods. Ideally, the contractor should assume the burden of tracing the lost shipment and/or replacing the damaged goods. The organization also may want to add a provision stating that the goods will be replaced within a certain period of time and reserve the right to replace the goods through other means at the contractor's expense.

Expediting and Tracing

Expediting occurs if the buyer wishes to accelerate the agreed-upon delivery time. Expediting differs from routine follow-up or checking to determine if the order will be received as expected. Depending on the goods that are en route, the shipment may be highly critical. For example, a repair part is being shipped for the water department and is now needed sooner than originally anticipated. The procurement staff or supplier then makes arrangements with the carrier, either before shipment, or at some stopping point, to adjust the delivery time.

Tracing occurs when the buyer wishes to follow the shipment during transport. Goods may be transported via multiple modes, which require a detailed understanding of how the various carriers handle their freight. Most often, the procurement professional can request the bill of lading, which will contain a unique number allowing the shipment to be traced. There should be a provision within the contract on how shipment tracing will be provided. The public agency should have a supplier contact person to perform this function and provide the shipping status within an agreed-upon time. A common turnaround time for this information is within 24 hours. When the supplier's representative attempts to trace a shipment, they need the following, at a minimum: (a) bill of lading; (b) description of material; and (c) date shipped.

Considered the most important transportation document, the bill of lading is the contract for transportation between the shipper and the carrier, which dictates the responsibilities and rights of both parties (Cavinato, 1982). The bill of lading is normally prepared by the shipper's logistics or traffic department but is legally issued by the carrier. U.S. government bills of lading (GBL) are used when government supplies, materials or personal property are transferred. Commercial carriers use their own forms, but they are standardized by industry and are generally negotiable. A negotiable or "order" bill of lading allows title or ownership of a shipment to be endorsed over to another party other than the original receiver. If a non-negotiable or "straight" bill of lading is issued, however, goods are consigned directly to the receiver and are generally delivered by the carrier without surrender of the bill of lading.

Force Majeure

Force majeure is a French term that refers to conditions that may occur that are outside of the control of either party. Circumstances that might prevent the supplier from performing in accordance with the contract include floods, earthquakes, tornadoes or even war. Because the supplier has neither fault nor control in such instances, the buyer cannot penalize the supplier for non-performance. If a critical shipment was a week late due to a snowstorm during which no normal transportation could get through, the organization would need to make whatever arrangements it could to address the material shortage. They would do so at their own cost because the supplier cannot be held liable. If a force majeure clause is not included in the contract, a legal action still may result on the basis that the clause should be implied under the Doctrine of Commercial Frustration (Hinkelman, 2000).

Length of Contract

The length of time an agreement is in place is referred to as the contract term. This is established up front in the contracting process and should be carefully considered. Generally, a long-term contract is going to secure the most competitive rates because suppliers find such guaranteed business very attractive. If a certain shipping company knows they have an organization's business for three years, they will likely do all they can to submit a favorable offer. A short-term contract may result in higher pricing and fewer concessions.

...a long-term contract is going to secure the most competitive rates because suppliers find such guaranteed business very attractive.

It is a good idea to consider renewals or extensions of the original contract. Often, organizations make initial contract awards and then consider renewals on an annual basis. This is a favorable strategy for the organization, as it will serve as an incentive for the supplier to perform well. Knowing that additional business in on the line may help keep the organization's deliveries a priority and on time.

Demurrage and Detention

When a buyer keeps a train car longer than the parties have agreed upon, the carrier can assess a demurrage charge. *Demurrage* is like rent and is a monetary amount that the buyer is obligated to pay for such retention. Imagine that an organization purchased a carload of fertilizer. The carrier dropped the delivery at the organization's warehouse with the understanding that the agency will have two days to unload it. After that time, the rail car will be scheduled for pickup so that the carrier can transport other shipments. If the organization experiences a delay in unloading the goods and keeps the trailer a third day, the carrier will bill for demurrage. This will be an additional charge and increase the cost of the original delivery.

Detention refers to the holding of a motor carrier's driver, truck, trailer or railroad container beyond a specified time period. Excessive holding may result in detention charges being assessed to the consignor or consignee. The consignor is the party that ships the goods, while the consignee is the person or company (usually the buyer) to whom the goods are to be delivered.

During international shipments, delays in clearing goods through Customs can also result in detention charges. In this situation, demurrage applies to the cargo, while detention generally applies to the equipment (Hinkelman, 2000).

Because demurrage and detention are issues that will have a financial impact on the buyer, they need to be clearly spelled out in the agreement. What are the grace periods, if any, for the organization, and what charges will be assessed if those periods are surpassed? Having these terms agreed upon can avoid much discussion and debate at a later time.

Conflicts and Disputes

Despite everyone's best efforts and intentions, inevitably, disputes arise during contract performance. It could be a disagreement over a delivery schedule, a difference over a freight bill, or countless other issues. The goal of each party should be to resolve the conflict in some mutually acceptable manner. When conflicts within the supply chain arise, they can be resolved basically in three ways: (a) litigation, (b) acceptance, and (c) negotiation (Hutchins, 2002).

Normally, litigation is the least preferred option, as it relies on attorneys and judges to settle the differences. It is an expensive and usually time-consuming process. Additionally, it often results in ill will between the parties for years to come. Some disputes will inevitably wind up in the courts. Recognition and acceptance of the issue is another approach. Unwillingness to accept that a conflict exists can lead to larger, long-term issues. The ideal approach would be to negotiate the differences between the parties. By using accomplished negotiation skills, the procurement professional can reach a settlement that is acceptable to both parties without litigation. A resolution that leaves both parties feeling content is referred to as "win-win."

The standard contract used by an organization may list arbitration or mediation as possible methods to settle a dispute. Procurement professionals should be aware of these formal contract requirements and should be a part of establishing such requirements. They should also attempt to resolve differences at the operational level so that contract performance can continue for the organization.

Package Delivery Services

While contracting for large or complex shipments via motor carriage or rail freight is important, the need for package delivery services should not be overlooked in the public sector. Particularly for small agencies, the use of carriers like UPS and FedEx for small package delivery may comprise the largest portion of their shipping expenditure. A local fire authority, for instance, may need small parts delivered on a daily basis, so focusing on package delivery services would be beneficial.

Cost and service are prime areas of consideration when contracting for package delivery. The corporate rates for national delivery companies are quite competitive, but it may be advantageous for small organizations to employ a separate contract for these services. This is an ideal area for utilizing a cooperative contract awarded by a larger agency. Many state procurement offices issue requirements contracts for such services that are available to governmental organizations throughout the area. In these cases, set rates are negotiated and need to be monitored. Routine monitoring by the procurement professional can help provide valuable cost control for the organization.

The organization should be familiar with the terms of the contract so that the service aspect can be monitored. Service factors such as delivery time, shipment tracking, and package "will calls" should be addressed. Knowing the services required of the shipping company, and holding them responsible for those requirements, is the key for small and large organizations. In addition to national firms like UPS and FedEx, there are also many local companies that provide package deliveries. These smaller, local companies can have a niche in public contracting, as they can offer a viable option for procurement professionals. Like other service and commodity areas, the competitive environment within this industry can help ensure favorable pricing and services. Package delivery providers will continue to play a valuable role for government in meeting freight transportation needs.

Conclusion

The transportation contract is an important instrument in public procurement. It includes terms and conditions that protect an organization's interests during the shipment of its goods. Regardless of which solicitation method is used, the resulting contract should be thorough, sound, and include certain provisions. Pricing and price changes are important, but so are contract terms and renewals. When something does go wrong during transit, areas such as shipment tracing, damages, and disputes can all come to the forefront. While each contract situation is unique, many issues remain consistent whether the contract is for motor, rail, or air transport. Agreements with freight forwarders, brokers, or third-party logistics providers need careful attention. In addition to performing their own research and using their own expertise, public procurement professionals should consider the use of transportation consultants to assist in the negotiation process (Gentry, 1991).

The ability to negotiate is a key skill in the public sector. Whether it is utilized during supplier selection or after contract award, it can be a valuable tool. Certain techniques can be employed to help ensure a favorable result for the procurement professional's organization. Being prepared at the onset of negotiations, even developing a negotiation plan, can mean the difference between success and failure. Laying the internal groundwork and developing objectives and desired outcomes can help all agency representatives operate as a team. Once a verbal agreement is reached between the parties, a written agreement should be drafted by the organization.

Today's procurement professionals need to be versed in contracting for services and be able to negotiate when needed. This can help ensure that the organization's goods arrive in the right condition, at the right price, and at the right time. As logistics services such as transportation continue to be outsourced by the government, the need to develop strong, detailed contracts will continue to be a requirement of the procurement professional.

References

Cavinato, J. L. (Ed.). (1982). *Transportation—Logistics dictionary.* Washington, DC: The Traffic Service Corporation.

Dawson, R. (1999). *The secrets of power negotiation, second edition.* Franklin Lakes, NJ: Career Press.

Duffy, R. J. (1999, March). Logistics: A custom link. *Purchasing Today, 10*(3).

Gentry, J. J. (1991). *Purchasing's involvement in transportation decision making.* Tempe, AZ: Center for Advanced Purchasing Studies.

Hinkelman, E. G. (2000). *Dictionary of international trade* (4th ed.). Novato, CA: World Trade Press.

Hutchins, G. (2002). *Supply management strategies for improved performance.* Portland, OR: Working It, LLC.

Konezny G. P., & Beskow, M. J. (1999). *Third party logistics: Improving global supply chain performance.* Minneapolis, MN: Piper Jaffray Equity Research.

Leenders, M. R., & Flynn, A. E. (1995). *Value driven purchasing.* New York: AMACOM, American Management Association.

National Association of State Procurement Officials (NASPO). (2001). *Survey of state and local government purchasing principles and practices.* Lexington, KY: NASPO.

National Institute of Governmental Purchasing, Inc. (NIGP) (2002). *Dictionary of purchasing terms* (5th ed.). Herndon, VA: NIGP.

National Institute of Governmental Purchasing, Inc. (NIGP) (2004). *The Legal Aspects of Public Purchasing.* Herndon, VA: NIGP.

Stroh, M. B. (2002). *Negotiation 101.* Available from www.logistics.ws/negotiation.htm.

Chapter 6

International Transportation

Global trade is a fact of life. Manufacturers can produce goods around the world and rely on fast transportation to move those goods from one country to another. Foreign trade continues to rise. If an organization is considering buying from foreign suppliers, there should be a clear understanding of the issues involving logistics and transportation. Because the distance goods travel from the supplier to the buying organization is longer, the inventory decisions will be affected. While the basic modes of transportation are the same, certain carriers and third parties specialize in international shipments to the United States. The legal environment must also be considered. While many nations have deregulated their own transportation systems, regulations, in most instances, remain strict between countries. Agreements among countries may also be negotiated through bilateral agreements, but additional paperwork will be involved.

Why Buy Global?

There are many reasons for buying from global suppliers, but most purchasing officers do so because they feel they are getting more value for the dollar. Leenders, Fearon, Flynn, and Johnson (2002) list 10 reasons to purchase from a foreign supplier; six of these specifically apply to government procurement.

1. Lower overall prices. Prices may be lower because of lower labor costs, better exchange rates, and more efficient equipment and processes. Suppliers may also focus production on specific products to gain economies of scale. Tariffs in many instances have been reduced keeping the overall cost, including logistics-related costs, down.

2. Quality, although not better, may be more consistent because suppliers own newer and better equipment, with better quality control systems in place and an emphasis on zero defects (producing products right the first time).

3. Items may not be available domestically, including raw materials such as palladium and manufactured goods such as computer printers or video equipment.

4. International suppliers may provide faster delivery than domestic suppliers or offer domestic inventory control until the product is ready for use. For example, aluminum ore (bauxite) is imported from Australia rather than the western U.S. and is brought to the eastern U.S. where it is processed. The cost to move it 10,000 miles by ocean freight is actually *less* than the 2000 miles it would travel by rail across the United States (Bloomberg et al., 2002).

5. Better technical service may be offered if the international supplier has a good distribution network in place.

6. Advanced technology may be offered by international suppliers, especially in primary metals such as steel.

Similar to the selection of domestic suppliers, global suppliers should be reliable and responsible. An organization may be too small to manage the local suppliers and also qualify new global suppliers. When the dollar value of the contract is high, site visits are important even though they may be expensive and time-consuming. Some challenges identified in selecting global sources include:

- Language barriers
- Quality control
- Long lead-times
- Complex logistics
- Political instability

- Time differences
- Inflexible quantity requirements
- Shipping costs
- Currency exchange risks
- Import duties (Anonymous, 2000).

A poll taken by *Purchasing* Magazine in 2000 showed that even small organizations plan to expand global sourcing. Eighty percent of those who bought offshore said they had increased buying from foreign suppliers, and 64% planned to see a similar increase in the next five years.

Trends in the Global Marketplace

There are several trends occurring in the global marketplace that specifically relate to logistics. First, there has been growth in world trade almost one and one-half times that of the world economy (United Nations, 2001). As shown in Table 5, both exports and imports have continued upward with the exception of 2001 when the United States experienced a recession. Logistics has made this possible through better planning and information technologies, improved trade agreements among nations, and faster means of transportation.

Period	Trade Balance ($ millions)	Exports ($ millions)	Imports ($ millions)
1980	($19,500)	$225,700	$245,300
1985	(117,700	218,800	336,500
1990	(101,700	393,600	495,300
1992	(84,500)	448,200	532,700
1993	(115,600)	465,100	580,700
1994	(150,600)	512,600	663,300
1995	(158,700)	584,700	743,400
1996	(170,200)	625,100	795,300
1997	(181,500)	689,200	870,700
1998	(229,800	682,100	911,900
1999	(328,800)	695,800	1,024,600
2000	(436,100)	781,900	1,218,000
2001	(411,400)	730,900	1,142,300

Table 5. *U.S. Trade in Goods, 1980-2001*

Source: U.S. Department of Commerce. (2001). *U.S. aggregate foreign trade data: Table 3*. Washington, DC: International Trade Administration. Available from www.ita.gov.

The United States has several large trading partners, accounting for more than 70% of all imports and almost 65% of all exports. As shown in Table 6, Canada, Mexico, and Japan are the United States' largest partners in both imports and exports. China also accounts for more than $120 billion, and trade will most likely continue to grow.

Country	Total Trade Dollars ($ millions)
Canada	$380,690
Mexico	232,940
Japan	184,240
China	121,520
Federal Republic of Germany	89,270
United Kingdom	82,190
Republic of Korea	57,380
France	50,190
Taiwan	51,540
Italy	33,740

Table 6. *Top 10 U.S. Trading Partners, 2001*

Source: U.S. Department of Commerce. (2001). *Top trading partners.* Washington, DC: U.S. Census Bureau. Available from www.census.gov.

A second trend is the growth of containers used in international trade. Containers are moved on some form of cargo vessels, carrying primarily semi-manufactured and manufactured products. From 1996 to 1999, cellular container ships for the world increased an average of 8% per year and 12% if measured in 20-foot equivalents (TEUs) (United Nations, 2001). Five ship liners control more than 25% of world capacity.

Container-ship operators are increasing the use of vessel-sharing agreements. Vessel-sharing agreements involve two or more carriers that share space on one or more vessels. The agreements range from space charter arrangements to more complex carrier alliances. The advantages are expanded geographic coverage, better utilization of ships, and a reduction in average costs. As shown in Table 7, about 36% of world capacity could be attributed to five vessel-sharing agreements.

Agreement Name	Carriers Involved*	# of Vessels	TEUs
Grand Alliance	6	90	340,063
Maersk/Sea-Land	5	111	334,429
New World Alliance	6	80	308,070
Hanjin/Tricon	9	66	223,924
K-Line/Yangming	4	38	111,665
Total	30	385	1,318,151

*Includes regional partners

Table 7. *Vessel Sharing Agreements, 1997*

Source: U.S. Department of Transportation. (1999). *Maritime Trade & Transportation.* Washington, DC: Bureau of Transportation Statistics.

A third trend related to the growth of containers has been an increase in intermodalism—the joint use of two or more modes in a shipment. For example, truck trailers may be moved on rail flatcars, also known as trailer on flatcar (TOFC) or piggybacking. Containers may also be moved on rail flatcars (COFC) or on ships. The Department of Defense, for example, has used an intermodal system to move and store unit equipment and supplies with small connectable containers called Quad cons (Transportation Research Board and National Research Council, 2000). Four Quad cons can be connected to form one 20-foot equivalent unit container, or TEU. Broken down, they can be loaded onto the backs of trucks. They also utilize intermodal rail cars. Ammunition and other supplies are moved intermodally from depots and warehouses onto the battlefield.

A fourth trend is the lowering of trade barriers among nations. The World Trade Organization (WTO) replaced the General Agreement on Tariffs and Trades (GATT), an unofficial trade organization, in 1995 and has been a catalyst for improved trade relations. Made up of nation members, the WTO is the only international organization dealing with rules of trade between countries (www.wto.org). Membership includes 144 nations, and they function to provide a forum for trade negotiations, handle trade disputes, monitor National trade policies, and provide technical and trade assistance to developing nations. The WTO's guiding principles are that the trading system should (a) function without discrimination between trading partners; (b) be freer, with barriers coming down through negotiation; (c) be predictable, without arbitrary tariffs or other non-tariff barriers; (d) be more competitive, eliminating export subsidies, product dumping, and similar practices; and (e) be more beneficial to less developed countries.

...the WTO is the only international organization dealing with rules of trade between countries...

Greater economic integration among neighboring nations has been a fairly recent occurrence, where there is a pooling of resources to provide a larger marketplace for member nations and producers. Some of these agreements include the North American Free Trade Agreement (NAFTA), the European Union (EU), Mercosur in Latin America, and Association of Southeast Asian Nations (ASEAN) in Asia. Advantages of these agreements include the reduction of red tape, less documentation, and freer movement of traffic at national borders.

International Transportation Choices

Ocean Transportation

Ocean transportation is the most important and most often used form of transportation for international shipments. As shown in Figure 7, capacity in gross tons increased during the 1990s, growing an average of 3.1% per year.

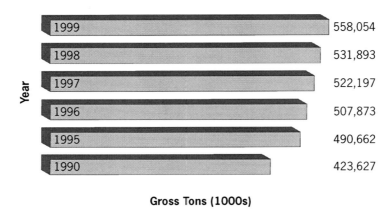

Year	Gross Tons (1000s)
1999	558,054
1998	531,893
1997	522,197
1996	507,873
1995	490,662
1990	423,627

Figure 7. *World capacity of merchant fleets, 1990-1999*

Source: United Nations. (2001). *Review of developments in transport and communications in the ESCAP region 1996-2001* (p.88). Available from www.unescap.org.

Ocean vessels are typically used to move lower-valued products with a high density. Sea freight is generally categorized by type, including (a) dry bulk—coal, grains, ores, fertilizers, alumina, bauxite, sugar; (b) liquid bulk—petroleum, chemicals, fertilizers; (c) containerized non-bulk items; and (d) general, non-containerized, non-bulk items.

There are several forms of service offered with distinctive differences. *Liners*, often called freighters, carry mostly general cargo and offer space to any shipper. They offer regularly published schedules with specific routes, sailing whether they are full or not. They charge set tariffs or rates depending on the cargo type, weight and distance shipped. Tariffs may be published on their web site or through an independent party. A large volume of their tonnage is dedicated to container ships or a combination of containers and other cargo. Large steamship companies generally own liners with many belonging to *shipping conferences*.

Shipping conferences, formed around 1870, are associations of shipping lines offering service for a given sea route on conditions agreed upon by the members (Branch, 1989). Considered semi-monopolistic in nature, they were originally started to create a bond between shippers and carriers: shippers would use only conference vessels, and conferences agreed to charge lower rates than if a shipper used a non-conference carrier. Conference members are also allowed to *pool* or share vessels to eliminate competition and reduce costs. If a conference member uses a U.S. port, *service contracts* may be negotiated with shippers. With a service contract, the shipper agrees to ship a minimum volume of cargo, usually defined in TEUs— the number of 20-foot containers. Set rates are based on an intermodal, point-to-point or port-to-port basis. The carrier must guarantee regular service and specialized equipment over a set period of time. Today, service contracts must be filed over the Internet with the Federal Maritime Commission (FMC) (www.fmc.org). About half of all cargo moves are under service contracts and this number is expected to increase (Harrington, 1999).

The conference system has weakened since the United States passed the Ocean Shipping Reform Act of 1998 (OSRA) (Gourdin, 2001). As of May 1999, liner carriers can now enter into confidential service contracts. However, carriers may not charge anything other than their published tariff rates or service contract rates. Groups of shippers can also enter into service contracts, although non-vessel-operating common carriers (NVOCCs) are prohibited from doing so. While carriers retain their antitrust immunity on agreements filed with the FMC, they are still required to meet the common carrier obligation of the Shipping Act of 1984. Tariff filing with the FMC was eliminated and replaced by electronic publication through private services or Internet sites. During the first year of OSRA, more than 46,000 new service contracts were filed with the FMC, an increase of 124% over 1998 and a strong indicator of their popularity. Many carriers have also left their conferences, setting their own rates and relying on vessel-sharing agreements.

A second form of carriage is the *charter ship*, where vessel owners contract with a shipper/ charterer for a specific voyage, known as *voyage charters*, or for a specific period of time, known as *time charters*. The charterer pays for all operating costs during the contract period, and the vessel owner provides the crew. A charterer can carry any cargo other than that which is prohibited by the contract.

Bareboat charters, also known as *demise* charters, are a third option. Full control of the vessel is transferred to the charterer, who hires the crew, pays all operating expenses, and accepts full responsibility for the vessel. Ship brokers generally make arrangements for charters, keeping track of the location and status of ships. The shipper contacts the broker who negotiates a price that includes a broker commission.

Finally, private ocean carriers owned by the shipper is an option. Private carriage is often used to lower costs or have more control.

International Airlines

Movement of air freight vis-à-vis air transportation has become increasingly popular with the advent of more frequently scheduled flights that reduce international transportation times to as little as one to two days. Federal Express, the United Parcel Service, and others have also entered the market, offering door-to-door delivery and other logistical services. High dollar, low weight items are still most commonly moved by air.

International airlines are subject to various government regulations. Regulation between any two countries is still relatively strict in most cases. Movements may be governed by *bilateral agreements*—economic alliances between two countries only. These agreements are negotiated by the countries' governments rather than by the airlines. The United States, for example, has negotiated "open-skies" agreements with Germany, Canada, the Netherlands, and Singapore, which allow free access into the other countries' international air markets. Specific airports, a carrier from each nation to provide service on the route, and the amount of service provided are negotiated in advance between the two countries. This will surely change as countries form multinational economic organizations like the European Union (EU). In the EU, for example, all domestic markets are open to any EU carrier if it chooses to serve them (Gourdin, 2001).

Intermodalism

Intermodalism is an important trend in the international movement of freight. Intermodalism refers to the movement of containers (one mode) using at least one other mode of transportation. A multimodal bill of lading, or combined transport bill of lading, may be used to cover the multiple movements, thus decreasing the amount of paperwork.

The options to shippers include (a) all water transportation, (b) *mini land bridge*, (c) *land bridge*, and (d) *micro-bridge*. A mini land bridge, or *mini-bridge*, is the shipment of goods from one country's port to a second country's port, with overland transportation in the first country. For example, a shipment may originate from a Long Beach, California, port, move across the United States via rail to New York, and then move via ship to its final destination of La Havre, France. A *land bridge* is a shipment between two countries, with overland transportation in a third country. For example, goods are shipped from China to Rotterdam, Netherlands, via the United States, where the containers are unloaded in Seattle, Washington, transported via air to New York City, and then on to Rotterdam. Lastly, a *micro-bridge* is a shipment from one country's port to another country's inland destination or vice versa. For example, containers are shipped from Viet Nam to Dallas, unloaded in San Francisco onto rail cars for transport to their final destination.

Intermediaries

A number of third parties, or intermediaries, are important to the successful shipment of goods from one country to another. *Foreign freight forwarders* are a good option for those new to international buying. They hire people with expertise in all areas of global shipping to help those organizations too small to have a department devoted to international issues. Foreign freight forwarders typically consolidate small shipments into container-size lots or to fill an entire ship. They also fill a needed role in advising shippers on the best means to package and ship goods as well as how to assure their shipment meets all statutory and maritime obligations (Branch, 1989). Their fees are earned through document preparation or commissions charged to carriers. They also perform other functions, including:

- Rate quotes
- Chartering or booking vessels
- Customs clearance
- Tracing and expediting shipments
- Arranging for inland transportation service (Coyle, Bardi, & Langley, 1996).
- Document preparation
- Obtaining cargo insurance
- Paying freight charges
- Language translation; and

An *air freight forwarder* performs similar functions to foreign freight forwarders but for air freight only. They may prepare and present documentation, trace and expedite shipments, publish tariffs, issue air waybills, and accept responsibility for damaged shipments.

Non-vessel-operating common carriers focus on the consolidation of small shipments into containers headed to inland destinations. They will book container space on steamship liners at reduced rates and then resell that space to small shippers, giving them the price advantage of being a large shipper. Since the passage of OSRA, U.S.-owned NVOCCs are required to be licensed. They must file a bond or provide proof of financial responsibility in an amount determined by the FMC.

> *A number of third parties, or intermediaries, are important to the successful shipment of goods from one country to another.*

Shippers associations are another means to move small shipments for the members through consolidation. As nonprofit cooperatives, these associations are able to negotiate a lower rate because of the larger volume shipment and pass that rate on to the member. Members also avoid the markups charged by the other intermediaries mentioned earlier. Because members are acting collectively, they generally receive better service from carriers.

Customs house brokers, licensed by the Department of the Treasury, provide a service to shippers by assuring all documentation required for a shipment is complete and accurate for entrance into the United States. The advent of computers has made their job much easier, reducing the time needed for clearance through customs and, thus, reducing overall lead times on international shipments.

Ship brokers are sales and marketing representatives for charter vessel owners, acting as middlemen between ship owners and shippers. A ship broker keeps track of port calls or when ships will be in port, and then matches this with the needs of a shipper.

Ship agents represent the vessel owner while the ship is in port. The agent arranges for several things, including the ship's arrival, berthing, any clearances needed, unloading and loading, and payment of port fees.

Terms of Sale and Documentation

Terms of sale include when and where the actual transfer of goods (i.e., trade terms), payment, legal title, and responsibility for insuring the goods takes place. Trade terms most widely used internationally are known as Incoterms, published by the International Chamber of Commerce in Paris (Hinkelman, 2000) and revised in 2000. They provide a set of uniform rules for international transactions, including defining the risks, costs and obligations of both buyer and seller. It is important to learn these terms because there are variations in meaning from our domestic terms. While not law, Incoterms should be included in the contract to avoid future misunderstandings and disputes. If there are disputes, the courts or arbitrators will use the sales contract as one point of reference in addition to whoever has possession of the goods and whether payment has been made. There are thirteen Incoterms grouped into four categories (Table 8). Group E contains only one term, ex works, which indicates the seller makes the goods available at its premises for pickup by the buying firm/importer. Group F includes three terms that determine at what point the seller is responsible for delivering the goods (carrier, port, or rail-side), while Group C sets the terms for when additional costs of risk or damage are transferred to the buyer. Group D terms are used when the seller is responsible for delivery of goods and defines the point of arrival. The most commonly used terms by government agencies would likely fall into Group D. More detailed information can be found in Hinkelman's *Dictionary of International Trade*.

Group	Meaning	Incoterm	Meaning to Buyer	Applicable Mode
E	Goods available at point of departure	EXW (Ex Works)	Buyer contracts and pays transportation; greatest responsibility	All modes
F	Seller delivers goods to specified carrier	FCA (Free carrier-named place)	Buyer contracts and pays transportation; seller delivers goods to carrier	All modes
		FAS (Free alongside ship-named port)	Buyer contracts and pays transportation; seller delivers goods to loading port	Ocean, inland waterways
		F.O.B. (Free on board–named port)	Buyer contracts and pays transportation; seller delivers goods to ship's rail side	Ocean, inland waterways
C	Seller contracts and pays for movement of goods and none to some costs	CFR (Cost and freight)	Seller contracts and pays transportation, delivers to designated port	Ocean, inland waterways
		CIF (Cost, insurance, and freight)	Seller contracts and pays transportation and marine insurance past ship's rail of designated port	Ocean, inland waterways
		CPT (Carriage paid to named port of destination)	Seller contracts and pays transportation, delivers goods to named port; buyer pays all other costs	All modes
		CIP (Carriage and insurance paid to named port of destination)	Seller contracts and pays for transportation and insurance, delivers goods to named port; buyer pays all other costs	All modes
D	Seller contracts and pays for movement and some to all costs involved	DAF (Delivered at frontier-named place)	Seller pays for transportation to designated point, not yet cleared for import	All modes
		DES (Delivered ex ship-named port of destination)	Seller pays for transportation to designated port, not yet cleared for import	Ocean, inland waterways
		DEQ (Delivered ex quay-named port of destination)	Seller pays for transportation to designated wharf, not yet cleared for import	Ocean, inland waterways
		DDU (Delivered duty unpaid-named port of destination)	Seller pays for transportation to destination; buyer responsible for import, all other costs	All modes
		DDP (Delivered duty paid-named port of destination)	Seller pays for transportation to destination, cleared for import, but not unloaded	All modes

Table 8. *Summary of Incoterms*

Documentation specific to international shipments is also common when importing goods into the United States and can be overwhelming, requiring absolute accuracy to avoid shipment delays. Government and industry are both working to simplify the process, thereby reducing transaction costs and time. NAFTA and the EU have both aligned documents with similar information to speed the transportation of goods between member nations. With increased use of either traditional or web-based electronic data interchange (EDI), the number of paper documents should also diminish. U.S. Customs is also streamlining the process, working toward a completely paperless environment by 2010. It uses the Automated Manifest System (AMS) by which shippers may notify Customs of inbound air, sea, or rail shipments before they arrive at a U.S. point of entry. Customs then notifies shippers as to which ones need to be inspected, and those shipments can be designated before arrival, thus, speeding up the process. Once the goods are inspected, they receive electronic clearance. About 90% of all inbound ocean bills of lading are now transmitted electronically (www.customs.ustreas.gov). Another advance is the Automated Brokerage Interface (ABI), designed for messaging between U.S. Customs and intermediaries to facilitate a shipment's clearance.

...letters of credit (LCs) are important in international transactions, protecting both the buyer and seller.

In addition to the shipping documentation required, *letters of credit* (LCs) are important in international transactions, protecting both the buyer and seller. A letter of credit, also known as *documentary credit*, is a bank's written promise to pay the seller on behalf of the buyer for goods purchased. The bank acts as an intermediary, collecting payment from the buyer and sending it forward to the seller once proof is presented that the goods have been shipped and entitle the buyer to the goods upon arrival. A bill of lading provides evidence of shipment and title transfer. For example, Christie Manufacturing, located in North Carolina, wants to purchase a piece of equipment from Columbo Industries, located in Italy. Columbo Industries is not willing to ship the equipment without being paid in advance, nor does it want to ship C.O.D. because of fears that the equipment may be rejected. Christie Manufacturing has never had dealings with Columbo Industries and does not want to pay in advance. As a result, Christie Manufacturing has its bank issue a letter of credit. The letter states that the bank will honor a draft drawn against the bank in the agreed amount. The draft must include specified documents, such as the bill of lading, signed commercial invoice, packing documents, and insurance forms.

Packaging

Because internationally purchased goods are in transit longer and handled more frequently, they are more susceptible to poor weather conditions. Packaging can add considerable costs to global movements through the use of more material and labor. Labeling and marking requirements vary from country to country and are an additional expense. Labeling is regulated to provide product descriptions through set standards, enforce compliance with current product standards, and restrict and/or control the use of additives (Hall, 1992). Marking helps facilitate package identification through the use of certain numbers, letters, and symbols. Marking may include weight, height, invoice numbers, and transit instructions. The International Air Transport Association, the Inter-Governmental Maritime Consultative Organization, and the United Nations jointly published standards to gain more consistency (Bloomberg, LeMay, & Hanna, 2002).

Ports

The points where shipments are exchanged between water and land carriers are referred to as ports. They serve several functions, including:

- Entrance into a country
- Discharging the ship to shore
- Sorting goods
- Assessing duties
- Movement of goods from dock area to transportation network.

- Mooring of ships
- Checking goods
- Storage
- Loading onto vehicles

More than 37 U.S. ports serve hundreds of ships with 22,750 port calls each year. Additionally, four million containers move into the United States annually. The volume of trade has also grown, with combined exports and imports on liner ships totaling $485 billion in 2000 (World Shipping Council, 2001). Most cargo entering into the United States is then transferred to rail or truck for transport to its final destination. The World Shipping Council cited congestion at the marine terminal gate as a significant issue in the nation's busiest ports. Most of these problems occur because of truck and rail access to the terminal area. For railroads, bridge clearance or the distance from the railroad to the terminal may cause such problems. For trucks, roads connecting marine terminals with the national highway system are often inadequate.

The Port and Maritime Security Act of 2001 was enacted to tighten security at all U.S. ports. The Coast Guard has "implemented several measures to improve tracking vessels destined for U.S. ports" (World Shipping Council, 2002, p. 4) and other proposals have been submitted to the International Maritime Organization. A recommendation that all port facilities have a security plan approved by the government is included in one of the World Shipping Council's proposals. It is too early to determine other effects of the Act, but the World Shipping Council has also made several recommendations to Congress regarding shipment of containers, including:

- Sealing a container originating from or destined for the United States upon stuffing it and recording the seal number on all shipping documents;

- Setting standards for the seal;
- Recording the seal and its condition upon receipt of the container;
- Procedures for containers with missing, broken or tampered seals; and
- Requirement that no loaded container be stowed aboard a vessel unless the seal is intact and in conformance with set standards.

Conclusion

P ublic procurement professionals continue to expand buying into international markets and related transportation issues. Recent trends indicate that the amount of international trade will continue to increase in the foreseeable future. There are multiple components of international transportation that do not fall within the procurement professional's control, including infrastructure, legal, cultural differences, and political climate. The purchasing professional should consider these issues and others in buying transportation services. Intermediaries, including foreign freight forwarders and customs brokers, among others, can make these transactions easier.

References

Anonymous. (2000). Global sourcing to grow—But slowly. *Purchasing*.

Bloomberg, D. J., LeMay, S., & Hanna, J. B. (2002). *Logistics*. Upper Saddle River, NJ: Prentice Hall.

Branch, A. E. (1989). *Elements of shipping* (6th ed.). London: Chapman and Hall.

Coyle, J. J., Bardi, E. J., & Langley, C. J., Jr. (1996). *The management of business logistics* (6th ed.). Minneapolis/St. Paul, MN: West Publishing Company.

Gourdin, K. N. (2001). *Global logistics management.* Oxford, UK: Blackwell Publishers, Ltd.

Hall, R. D. (1992). *International trade operations* (2nd ed.). Jersey City, NJ: Unz and Company.

Harrington, L. H. (1999, January 5). A new era dawns. *Industry Week*.

Hinkelman, E. G. (2000). *Dictionary of international trade* (4th ed.). Novato, CA: World Trade Press.

Leenders, M. R., Fearon, H. E., Flynn, A. E., & Johnson, P. F. (2002). *Purchasing and supply management.* Boston: McGraw-Hill Irwin.

Transportation Research Board and National Research Council. (2000, February 23-26).

Conference proceedings 25—Global intermodal freight: State of readiness for the 21st century, Long Beach, California.

United Nations. (2001). *Review of developments in transport and communications in the ESCAP region 1996-2001*. Available from www.unescap.org.

World Shipping Council. (2001, May 23). Statement of Christopher Koch, President

World Shipping Council on Port and Maritime Transportation Congestion before the House Transportation and Infrastructure Committee. Available from www.worldshipping.org.

World Shipping Council. (2002, March 13). Testimony of Christopher Koch, President & CEO of the World Shipping Council Before the House Transportation and Infrastructure Committee. Available from www.worldshipping.org.

Chapter 7

Advances In Information Technology

As procurement continues to move away from simply processing transactions to a more strategic role of managing supplier relationships, the view of the organization becomes one of an *extended enterprise* of buyers, suppliers, intermediaries, and transportation carriers. Multiple organizations must be strategically aligned, focusing on specific market opportunities. Shared information among these individual organizations makes this concept of the extended enterprise and a true supply chain possible. Linking procurement directly to suppliers and transportation carriers allows for "real-time" responses to changes in market conditions. Availability of information also aids decision-making, helps reduce costs, and increases the responsiveness of a transportation network. Simply stated, information systems allow for planning, control, and matching of supply with demand in short timeframes. Today, computer software, hardware, the Internet, and other tools make information-sharing a reality.

Rethinking the Supply Chain and Information

A common visual conception of the supply chain is the link-and-mode model, as shown in Figure 8. Individual organizations are considered to work independently with order information and goods flowing from point to point. To increase speed and response time within the supply chain, Greis and Kasarda (1997) argue that a new way of thinking is required, viewing the chain as a set of interfaces between organizations, including transportation, that must be managed rather than a set of activities to be accomplished independently and sequentially (Figure 9).

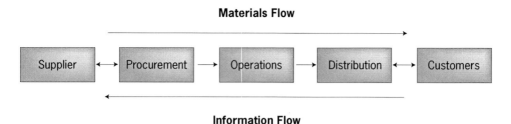

Figure 8. *Traditional view of the supply chain.*

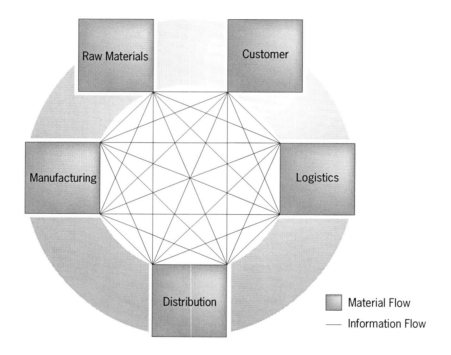

Figure 9. *New view of the supply chain.*

Instead of viewing activities sequentially, Greis and Kasarda (1997) state, "Information flows electronically around the collective enterprise in what can be called a transaction web" (p. 65). Several shipments from suppliers, for example, can be synchronized to arrive at the same time as required by the customer. Additionally, the customer, supplier, transportation carrier, and other intermediaries can regularly monitor information on the status of an order or shipment. Essentially, this is a movement beyond Electronic Data Interchange (EDI) to an electronic network of simultaneous connections with all partners necessary to transact business. From this connectivity comes something referred to as *economies of conjunction*, or the efficiencies and speed that are possible based on how organizations manage information and business transactions.

Economies of conjunction can be extended to logistics. Greis and Kasarda (1997) suggest that organizations should strive to develop a "logistics environment", which is time-sensitive, flexible, and collaborative. This environment is now possible because of real-time movement of information among partnering organizations. To achieve this, organizations need a transportation network consisting of multiple modes capable of moving products and materials without interruption based on customer requirements. A network of multimodal and intermodal transportation requires information access. All partners require electronic connectivity to access a shared information network. Figure 10 provides an example of how the information flows to support the relationship between supplier, buying organization, and carrier. Ideally, an integrated information systems infrastructure coordinates the information systems of each party—carrier, buying firm, and supplier.

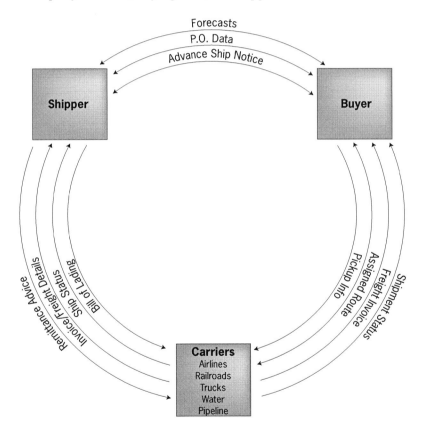

Figure 10. *Information flows.*

Source: Adapted from Scheff, S., & Livingston, D. B. (1991). *Computer integrated logistics: CIL architecture in the extended enterprise.* Southbury, CT: IBM Corporation and U.S. Transportation Industry Marketing.

Current Issues in Technology

C omputer Systems Corporation (CSC) (2001) annually surveys information executives on critical issues in information systems management. Table 9 provides a comparison of issues globally in the government/public sector versus respondents from all industries. As stated in the report, "More and more, people expect to be able to conduct their transactions with governments and public sector organizations electronically, as they do with such private businesses as banks and bookstores" (p. G1).

Top IS Management Issues Globally	Government (Percentage)	All Respondents (Percentage/Rank)
Optimizing Enterprise-wide IS Services	66.7%	64.8% (1)
Instituting Cross-functional Information Systems	66.7%	52.4% (8)
Organizing and Utilizing Data	65.6%	61.4% (3)
Protecting & Securing Information Systems	63.4%	55.3% (5)
Aligning IS and Corporate Goals	57.0%	54.2% (7)
Integrating Systems with the Internet	57.0%	42.4% (13)
Updating Obsolete Systems	54.8%	54.2% (6)
Optimizing Organizational Effectiveness	54.8%	62.6% (2)
Connecting to Customers, Suppliers, and/or Partners Electronically	49.5%	57.2% (4)
Capitalizing on Advances in Information Technology (IT)	47.3%	40.2% (15)

Table 9. *Top Issues in Information Systems*

Source: Computer Systems Corporation (CSC). (2001). 14th annual *critical issues of information systems management survey*. El Segundo, CA: CSC.

According to the survey findings (CSC, 2001), most of these factors appear to be related to supply chain matters. The area of greatest concern for both the government sector and industry as a whole is "optimizing enterprise-wide information systems services," with "instituting cross-functional information systems" ranking number two. Included in the top 10 issues was "connecting to customers, suppliers and/or partners electronically," although this issue was ranked much higher at number four for all respondents. In 2001, more than 65% of the government/public sector respondents saw an increase in their information systems budget, and 89% of new initiatives were related to Internet technologies. Respondents reported that currently, of the top five functions conducted with Internet technology, collaborative commerce was number two with supply chain ranked number five (Table 10). However, collaborative commerce is expected to move to number one with a higher percentage of planned technology projects for logistics. The government/public sector also reported that in 2001, 18.0% of external business was done electronically, including EDI, compared to 14.4% in 2000. This percentage was expected to jump to 23.2% in 2002.

Functions Conducted with Internet Technology	Current	Planned	Percentage
Employee Services/Intranet	38.2%	Collaborative Commerce	25.0%
Collaborative Commerce	21.4%	Back Office	23.2%
Front Office	17.8%	Employee Services/Intranet	21.8%
Back Office	14.3%	Front Office	21.4%
Supply Chain	10.9%	Logistics	18.2%

Table 10. *Functions Conducted with Internet Technology*

Source: Computer Systems Corporation (CSC). (2001). 14th annual *critical issues of information systems management survey.* El Segundo, CA: CSC.

From the transportation side, a study by Kerr (2001) reported survey results from 50 leading transportation companies. Respondents reported that they planned to make significant investments in (a) tracking and tracing software (88%); (b) company Internet sites (75%); and (c) back-office functionalities (75%) in an effort to provide visibility in the supply chain to shippers. More than half of all respondents also reported that investments would be made in the Intranet, e-documentation, revenue management technologies, and optimization technologies, including fuel and routes.

Information Technologies Today

There are multiple means to "stay connected" in the supply chain. While electronic data interchange (EDI) has been around for close to thirty years, the Internet has rapidly grown as a means of communication among supply chain partners.

Electronic Data Interchange

EDI, a staple in communications technology, has been defined as "the inter-organizational, computer-to-computer exchange of business documentation in a standard, machine-processable format" (Emmelhainz, 1992). Introduced in the 1970s, EDI improves the speed and accuracy of paper-based documents. During the 1990s, the use of EDI increased rapidly. The benefits of EDI include improved cash flows and productivity with reductions in the following:

- Document preparation
- Inventory
- Personnel costs
- Lead times
- Processing time
- Carrying costs
- Shipping errors
- Ordering costs (Johnson, Wood, Wardlow, & Murphy, 1999).

Transportation companies use EDI to replace paper shipping documents, including freight bills, bills of lading, shipment status, pick-up requests, and remittance advices.

While EDI will be around in the foreseeable future, another technology tool, extensible markup language (XML), is gaining in popularity and is expected to eventually replace EDI. XML allows organizations to send messages via the Internet with a Web browser. Industry groups, such as RosettaNet and Open Application Group, are developing standards and looking for ways to translate EDI messages into the XML format. XML is also more affordable for small to medium size organizations.

Internet

As noted by Christopher (1998), "The Internet provides a perfect vehicle for the establishment of the virtual supply chain" (p. 272). KPMG International (2000), in a study of 22 motor carriers, designed a model to categorize carriers based on their use of the Internet. Four stages of Internet usage were identified.

1. Marketing basic information, including services and executives;
2. Publishing pricing information and annual reports;
3. Creating two-way transactional flows with customers/partners, including information access, placing and changing orders; and
4. Conducting all business transactions and information-sharing with real-time shipment visibility, collaborative planning, and customer order management.

KPMG International found that most carriers fell into Stage 3. Frequently offered services have been found to include freight quotes, shipment tracking, pickup scheduling, and access to receipts or bills of lading, which streamline and cut costs from the typical shipment. However, according to Hannon (2001), some carriers have reported a lack of Internet access by customers. While the company may have access, the traffic department does not; so freight companies are looking to alternative systems. Extensions of the Internet include extranets and intranets.

Extranet

Extranets have been defined as "a portion of a corporate network (intranet) that is open to customers, business partners, and anyone to whom the corporation grants access" (Davydov, 2001, p. 267). The extranet has the advantage of opening company information to customers and partners. CSX, a Fortune 500 transportation company, provides customer access to their Transportation WorkstationNet (TWSNet) to track car or fleet locations in real time (Anonymous, 1998a). Customers can also check and time rail pickups and deliveries, review tariffs and negotiated rates, and view rail car shipment capacities and maintenance records. Additionally, rail car ordering is simplified, giving managers the ability to enter shipping instructions to CSX's order processing system.

Intranet

With many organizations opening up information access through extranets, transportation companies are placing a high priority on intranets. They have been described as "a private network inside a company or organization built by using Internet technologies" (Davydov, 2001, p. 269). Intranets provide information sharing with access to text-based documents and corporate databases from any desktop with a browser. Yellow Transportation, Inc., a Fortune 500 holding corporation for a family of companies specializing in freight transportation, uses the intranet to provide their Terminal Operating System, which shares operations best practices and provides forums, bulletin boards, and online chats.

There are some drawbacks to intranets. Information is available in a multitude of sources and in all kinds of formats. Published documents may also be presented in an unstructured way. As a result, finding relevant, accurate information may be difficult, requiring a search through several systems. As of now, there are no established standards for navigation. Information can be accessed through different methods, including Web browsers, e-mail clients, and groupware applications. There are generally no interfaces with online databases, such as enterprise resource planning (ERP) or customer relationship management (CRM) applications.

With many organizations opening up information access through extranets, transportation companies are placing a high priority on intranets.

As a result, companies are moving toward *exchange portals*, which improve access to and processing of information. Exchange portals, Web-based interfaces into an organizational network, organize information into context-specific areas to improve communication and the relationship between customer and partnering organizations (Davydov, 2001). There are also industry-based portals, which are used to increase communication among supply partners within a specific industry. For example, the automotive industry has created an exchange portal to exchange information on designs, bids, schedules, and commodities.

Wireless Technology

Wireless computing provides a mobile computing platform, ideal in the logistics and transportation industry. Local and regional delivery companies can use wireless technology to track packages, while trucking and transportation companies track vehicles and goods. For example, global positioning systems (GPS) are the basis for locating fleet vehicles in the trucking industry. Motor carriers can modify their route structures of the nearest truck to improve customer response time. Rail companies are using wireless computing to improve scheduling of services and sending arrival and departure information.

R&L Carriers, with a fleet of 9,400 tractors and trailers, serves 33 states across the United States, Canada, and Puerto Rico (www.sierrawireless.com). They now use a portable document capture system that includes a scanner, computer, and wireless access. Drivers transmit shipping documents or bills of lading to corporate headquarters in real time for immediate processing. Bills for shipments can be generated within a day versus a week under the old system. Shipment information is also posted on the company Web site, which allows customers and shippers continuous access to tracking data.

Remote Control Technology

To improve safety, Class I railroads in the United States have begun pilot testing remote control technology, which utilizes an on-board computer to operate locomotives based on signals received from ground employees. In the past, a ground employee directed traffic via radio or hand signals to the locomotive engineer. The Canadian National Railroad has used remote control technology since 1989, and yard accidents have been reduced by 70% (CSX, 2002).

Bar Coding

Bar codes, read by optical scanners, have had a major impact on logistics beginning in the 1970s. Used to identify incoming shipments, bar codes consist of a series of parallel black and white bars of varying width. The sequence translates into letters or numbers that represent information, including the shipment's origin, product type, place of manufacture, and product price (Coyle, Bardi, & Landley, 1996). Each industry has its own bar-code standards, which include the code "language," print quality, type of information included, and information format. Lack of common standards across industries is one of the biggest issues facing organizations.

Scanners emit light beams to read the bar codes and may be stationary, hand-held, or attached to the wrist or finger. Advantages of scanning include improved data accuracy, a reduction in receiving time, integration of data with inventory controls and databases.

Radio Frequency

Radio frequency (RF) is used to relay information between drivers or operators and a warehouse or port yard. Radio frequency identification (RFID) identifies trailers, tractors, or other equipment in a yard; monitors trailer status at a remote location; and identifies arriving and departing tractors and trailers at yard gates. RF data collection is used to communicate with the driver or other mobile personnel. The U.S. Army currently uses RFID to maintain complete visibility of ammunition at their depot in Crane, Indiana; from the time it leaves the gate until it arrives to the right unit (Anonymous, 1998a). RF tags are programmed with content information for each container of ammunition. Tagging allows the Army to track the containers and review the tag periodically at port of departure, holding yards, port of destination, and at the final arrival point to determine what is in a container. Bar codes are also attached to the shipment to notify the Army that a container has been loaded and is then forwarded to the receiver at the Ammunition Supply Point.

Planning Issues

Transportation companies are searching for new information technologies that will increase their productivity and improve customer service. A multitude of product offerings are available, making the choices challenging for both carrier and customer. To evaluate the information technology decision, some factors should be considered, including:

- What are the organization's requirements as well as those of the logistics channel?
- What will the technology do to improve coordination and integration of key logistics activities?
- What data will be required for implementation?
- Will employees accept the new technology? If not, what can be done to increase their acceptance?
- Does the organization have the financial resources to ensure a smooth implementation? (Coyle et al., 1996)

Conclusion

S ignificant advances have been made to improve communication within an organization and among supply chain partners. The improvements in technology have reduced uncertainties in the supply chain, making it easier to exchange information and track the movement of goods. A good information system will assist in the planning and decision making process but should be designed with an organization's specific needs in mind. While there have been major advances in technology in recent years, there are still opportunities for future improvements in performance through supply chain analysis techniques.

References

Anonymous. (1998a). Break your yard bottleneck. *Transportation and Distribution, 39*(2), 84-87.

Anonymous. (1998b, October 5). Transportation tracking in real time. *Information Week*, 20SS.

Anonymous. (2002). ADC news and solutions: EDI. *Modern Materials Handling, 57*(3), 59-61.

Christopher, M. (1998). *Logistics and supply chain management.* London: Prentice Hall.

Computer Systems Corporation (CSC). (2001). 14th annual c*ritical issues of information systems management survey.* El Segundo, CA: CSC.

Coyle, J. J., Bardi, E. J., & Langley, C. J., Jr. (1996). *The management of business logistics* (6th ed.). Minneapolis/St. Paul, MN: West Publishing Company.

CSX. (2002). *CSXT introduces remote control technology.* Available from www.csx.com.

Davydov, M. M. (2001). *Corporate portals and e-business integration.* New York: McGraw Hill.

Emmelhainz, M. A. (1992). *EDI a total management guide.* London: International Thomson Computer Press.

Greis, N. P., & Kasarda, J. D. (1997). Enterprise logistics in the information era. *California Management Review, 39*(4), 55-78.

Hannon, D. (2001, November 15). Logistics and the Internet: Internet connections make shipments more visible. *Purchasing Today.*

Johnson, J. C., Wood, D. F., Wardlow, D. L., & Murphy P. R., Jr. (1999). *Contemporary logistics.* Upper Saddle River, NJ: Prentice Hall.

Kerr, F. (2001). *Technology utilization and collaboration within the transportation industry.* Available from www. eyefortransport.com.

KPMG International. (2000). *Strategic directions in E-Transportation.* Unpublished paper.

Scheff, S., & Livingston, D. B. (1991). *Computer integrated logistics: CIL architecture in the extended enterprise.* Southbury, CT: IBM Corporation and U.S. Transportation Industry Marketing.

Chapter 8

Environmental Logistics Initiatives

Environmental concerns came to the forefront in the early 1990s in response to the demand from governments for environmentally friendly products and practices. As a result, a "cradle-to-grave" responsibility has emerged, with organizations making the commitment to be responsible for products throughout their life cycle (Weiskott, 2000). Logistics is at the heart of this movement, with organizations considering issues of recycling, reclamation, remanufacturing, refurbishing, and disposal of packaging and products. Product categories that must be considered in the process include obsolete materials, scrap, worn out or depleted equipment, and by-products (Young, 2000). The initiative must begin with the procurement process, as supply managers determine factors involved in the total cost of ownership of an item as it relates to logistics.

Environmental Definitions

Environmental approaches include *green logistics* and *reverse logistics*. The term green logistics is used more broadly to describe "efforts to measure and minimize the environmental impact of logistics activities" (Rogers & Tibben-Lembke, 2001, p. 130). Reverse logistics is more specialized, focusing on the movement of material back from the point it was consumed to its original point. Stock (1998) defined reverse logistics as "the role of logistics in product return, source reduction, recycling, materials substitution, reuse of materials, waste disposal and refurbishing, repair, and remanufacturing" (p. 20). However, there is some overlap in the two terms, as pointed out by Rogers and Tibben-Lembke and shown in Table 11.

Material	Reverse Logistics Activities	Overlap	Green Logistics Activities
Products	Returns to supplier Resale Salvage Reconditioning Refurbishing Reclaiming Donation Disposal to landfill	Recycling Remanufacturing	
Packaging	Refurbishing Reclaiming Salvage Landfill	Reusing Recycling	Reduction
Other			Cleaner air Noise reduction Mode selection

Table 11. *Reverse and Green Logistics Activities*

Source: Adapted from Schwartz, B. (2000). Reverse logistics strengthens supply chains. *Transportation and Distribution, 41*(5); and Rogers, D., & Tibben-Lembke, R. (2001). An examination of reverse logistics practices. *Journal of Business Logistics, 22* (2).

Both reverse and green logistics cover recycling, remanufacturing, and the use of reusable packaging. For example, reusable packaging could include refillable bottles, reusable pallets, or reconditioned barrels. However, green logistics also refers to the reduction of packaging, air and noise emissions, and reducing the environmental impact of mode selection.

A recent study found that recycling materials, reducing consumption, and reusing materials whenever possible were the three most frequently used environmental strategies among U.S., Canadian, and European firms (Murphy & Poist, 2000). Additionally, three strategies expected to be implemented in the future by at least 30% of the respondents were the redesign of logistical systems to improve environmental efficiency, an increase in education and training, and rejecting suppliers that lacked environmental concerns.

Recent Trends

A 1999 report from the Environmental Protection Agency (EPA) summarized trends in municipal solid waste (MSW) since 1960, excluding biosolids, transportation equipment, hazardous materials, and construction debris. Results indicate that U.S. businesses today are doing a better job of materials and resource management. Pallets, for example, are being used multiple times before disposal rather than just once. There have also been increased recycling efforts. Americans with more disposable income are creating more waste. Total solid waste increased from 205.2 million tons in 1990 to 229.9 million tons in 1999, with estimates of 35% to 45% attributable to the commercial sector, which included schools, hospitals, prisons, industrial sites, and businesses.

Since 1960, per-capita disposal has increased, although recycling has also increased. Containers and packaging comprised the largest percentage of total MSW generated at 33.1%, with non-durable goods second at 27.1%. (Non-durable goods was a new category added in 1999 and includes VCRs, camcorders, personal computers and monitors, and telephones consumed for both commercial and personal use.) As shown in Figure 11, the most frequently recovered and recycled MSW, as a percentage of generation, are paper and paperboard, steel, and glass. Unfortunately, approximately 57% of all MSW is still taken to landfills, with 28% recovered/recycled and 15 percent combusted.

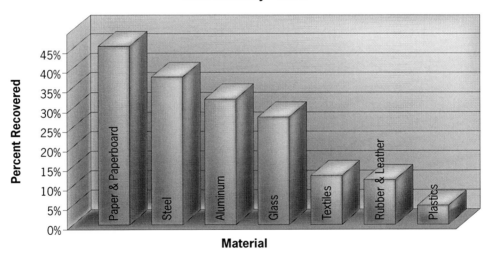

Figure 11. *Recovery of municipal solid waste, selected materials, 1999.*

Source: Adapted from U.S. Environmental Protection Agency (EPA). (1999b). *Municipal solid waste in the United States: 1999 final report* (p. 6). Washington, DC: EPA:

Total Cost of Ownership and Environmental Logistics Strategies

As organizations move toward more environmentally responsible practices, most have recognized that the total cost of an item goes beyond the initial buy to incorporate other activities, including final disposal—in other words, all costs tied to the life cycle of the product. The total cost of ownership (TCO), a purchasing methodology, considers the cost of all activities attached to a particular product. TCO has been defined as "the present value of all costs associated with a product, service, or capital equipment that are incurred over its expected life" (Menezes, 2001, p. 16). In addition to the actual purchase price, any costs related to the purchase and delivery of the product, use of the product, and disposition of the product when its useful life is over are a part of the total cost of ownership. Ellram (1993) broke down the total cost of a product or service to include three categories of costs, as presented in Figure 12.

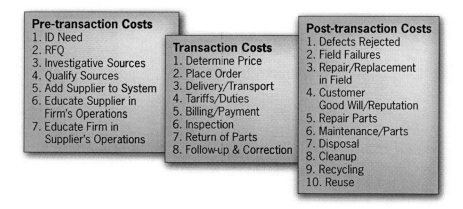

Figure 12. *Total cost of ownership—Categories and costs.*

Source: Adapted from Ellram, L. (1993). Total cost of ownership: Elements and implementation. *International Journal of Purchasing and Materials Management. 29*(4), 2-11; and Menezes, S. (2001, May). Calculating the total cost of ownership. *Purchasing Today*, 16-17.

Environmental logistics activities come into play in all stages of the total cost of ownership analysis (Tibben-Lembke, 1998). The Department of Defense, for example, took a number of steps in 1995 to develop contract specifications that applied environmentally preferred purchasing for the repair and maintenance of its parking lots (EPA, 1999a). Some of the costs included:

- Review of environmental certification programs for product standards;
- Independent product research of catalogs, directories and other sources to identify suppliers offering products with enhanced environmental features;

- Developing an RFP [Request for Proposal], which incorporated environmental attributes for packaging, plumbing fixtures, masonry, and building insulation; and

- Asking bidders to explain how they identified and purchased products with positive environmental attributes; how they would minimize construction waste and maximize debris recycling; and how their operating practices demonstrated environmental stewardship. (p. 12)

Transaction costs can be positively affected if a supplier with a... green logistics system has the ability to offer reconditioned or remanufactured products as a lower cost option.

Transaction costs can be positively affected if a supplier with a reverse or green logistics system has the ability to offer reconditioned or remanufactured products as a lower cost option. For example, Massachusetts started the Environmentally Preferable Products Procurement Program in the late 1980s to create demand for products that could be recycled (Fredette, 2001). In 2000, they estimated a savings of more than $260,000 through the purchase of remanufactured toner cartridges. Another consideration is the cost of a supplier offering to dispose of used products, which, when passed along to the buying organization, increases transaction costs. The supplier's order placement and billing system is also important, i.e., determining how quickly the organization will receive credit for returned goods so funds are freed up to purchase additional items.

If suppliers have integrated reverse logistics transportation with forward distribution costs, they may have improved buying power with their carriers, which can be passed on to the purchasing and supply management organization. Integration also improves transportation efficiencies because returned goods are carried on the backhaul. For example, seven of Chrysler's suppliers to their Belvedere plant use their delivery trucks to pick up protective closures used in packaging component parts on the backhaul (www.indstate.edu/recycle/9634.html). No additional transportation expense is incurred, and the closures are reusable up to 10 times. This process reduces disposal costs for Chrysler and cuts the cost of buying more protective closures for their suppliers.

The buying organization should determine the process for field failures. If the supplier has a reverse logistics system in place, instructions are generally provided for product return; therefore, convenience and satisfaction are improved. Products may also be repaired or remanufactured and returned to the customer. Repairing is the process of making a product operational again, but a complete analysis may not necessarily be done, and the product may not perform "as new." Remanufacturing means that a product has been completely disassembled and all parts examined for their condition, cleaned, repaired as necessary, tested, and reassembled to obtain optimal performance. The term "rebuilt" is used specifically in the automotive industry for vehicle parts. (More information is available from www.reman. org.) However, if the supplier does not have a reverse logistics system, the cost is borne as a separate expense by the buying organization. As a result, items will typically be stored until a large enough shipment is justified. However, storage can result in damage and/or obsolescence, thus adding to the total cost of ownership.

The product will eventually reach the point of disposal. Regulatory compliance may dictate disposal, as in the case of products containing asbestos or lead. Total costs may be recouped to some extent if the product or parts are salvageable. Additionally, some manufacturers may take back the product for a fee and dispose of it properly. The Canadian Government, for example, has created a checklist to help supply managers during the initial planning stages of a purchase to increase environmental responsibility (Fredette, 2001). Some issues that must be addressed regarding disposal of products or its parts include the ability to (a) reuse or reallocate; (b) resell to Canada's Crown Assets Distribution; (c) return to the supplier for recycling, reuse, or recovery; (d) recycle locally; or (e) contribute to a waste exchange program.

A Joint Effort

The City of Portland and Multnomah County, Oregon, have developed a partnership to implement a Sustainable Procurement Strategy. Realizing the cost of a good extends beyond initial procurement, they are looking beyond initial costs of the buy to all product costs including (a) extraction of raw materials; (b) handling; (c) shipping; (d) storage; (e) maintenance; (f) operations; and (g) disposal.

Their vision is to "promote actions which are environmentally and socially beneficial while also being economically intelligent." Starting in April 2002, Target Area Task Forces annually review and recommend changes for three to five commodities to be purchased for use in the next five years. The life cycle costs and benefits are considered, when possible, in the evaluation of goods and services.

Target Area Task Forces will review and collect additional information on a particular commodity and determine within a commodity group which products will receive attention. Feedback will then be collected from industry groups and subject matter experts on aspects of product life cycle, including suppliers. They will identify potential benchmarks for performance measurement and finish the process by making written recommendations on increasing sustainable procurement of the commodity.

Transportation and Location Issues

Transportation decisions are critical in recycling and reuse programs. Movement of used or recycled materials can be costly and greatly reduce the financial benefits a program offers. Often, organizations will choose the least expensive mode regardless of service levels. Rail is often chosen as the mode of choice over trucking strictly for cost reasons. Railroads move low-value commodities in high volumes at a low cost, with an added benefit of lower emissions of CO_2 and nitrous oxide. Railroads can also accommodate container shipments, thus reducing the need for trucks.

More efficient use of trucks, however, is another option. Using larger trucks for long-haul, direct transport results in fewer shipments and fewer emissions. Domestic sea shipping is a third less costly option that uses less fuel. Mitsubishi Electric of Japan, for example, moves large products, such as power generators and transformers, by sea.

There are also other alternatives that a procurement professional can consider. Chrysler was able to reuse protective closures at no additional transportation expense to the supplier. Suppliers may be willing to pay the freight to have certain items returned to them, as in the case of shipping containers. Schumacher Electric Corporation, a designer and manufacturer of electrical transformers, bales and recycles corrugated cartons that arrive daily (http://web.indstate.edu/recycle/9503.html). It then manufactures its own corrugated packaging parts for reuse as cushions, shelves, and partitions that fit inside cartons containing outgoing freight. This utilizes another option of reusing materials to avoid disposal and transportation costs.

A related consideration is the location for reverse logistics activities. Frequently, these sites are selected to minimize the costs of transportation. A centralized location may offer several benefits, including improved tracking of returns, customer satisfaction, safety, and time-saving. Transportation companies and other third parties may also offer customized reverse logistics programs.

Packaging and Movement of Hazardous Materials

A specialized form of environmental management practice is the packaging and movement of hazardous materials and waste. According to the Department of Transportation (DOT), there are approximately 300 million shipments per year of hazardous materials in the United States alone (NE DOT, 2000). Total tonnage is expected to increase by 2% per year, and movement by air or intermodally is estimated to grow three to four times faster than in other modes. Shippers are considered to have an early but critical impact on the movement of hazardous materials. Although only 5% of all inspections take place with the shipper, they have been identified as playing the biggest role in the safe transportation of hazardous materials to their destination. Caution should be exercised in selecting the carrier for shipment of hazardous materials. Shippers must verify that the selected carrier has the appropriate licensing and experience to transport the particular type of hazardous material being shipped. In addition, the shipper must assure that the selected disposal site for the final destination of the material is licensed to store/dispose that particular type of hazardous waste. The shipper must insist on receipt of a disposal certificate prior to releasing payment. Improper transportation or disposal of hazardous material may result in citations or penalties for the transporter and/or the shipper.

As generator of the hazardous material, the shipper may be responsible for that material regardless of any shipping arrangements or contracts. In cases where an agency lacks the resources to assure compliance with the many regulations for transportation and disposal of hazardous waste, selecting a third-party logistics expert who can address all transportation and disposal issues may be the best solution for assuring compliance. Always investigate the capability of any third-party logistics handler through thorough reference verifications.

Multiple regulations govern the handling, packaging, and transportation of goods identified as hazardous materials. Several sections of the United States Code of Federal Regulations (CFR) specific to the transportation, handling, and disposal of hazardous materials are found in Title 29, Title 40, and Title 49. Title 29 was created to protect the health and safety of employees that work with hazardous materials. The safe disposal of hazardous waste is covered under Title 40 and enforced by the EPA. Both the EPA and DOT have joint responsibility over regulating hazardous substances, defined as "severe pollutants to the environment" (*United States Code Annotated*, 1993, p. 239). Title 49 is the statute regulating the transportation of hazardous materials and is jointly enforced by the Research and Special Programs Administration and DOT's individual agencies governing air, rail, highways, and the Coast Guard. Title 49 covers five areas that are briefly described below.

...the EPA and DOT have joint responsibility over regulating hazardous substances...

Definition and Classification of Hazardous Materials. Several thousand of the most commonly transported hazardous materials are identified in the Hazardous Materials Table. They are divided into several classifications, including explosives, radioactive materials, gases, liquid and solid flammables, oxidizing materials, organic peroxides, corrosive materials, poisons and miscellaneous. Some hazardous materials may be designated as "forbidden" and may not be transported at all. Other materials may be not be transported by certain modes such as air transportation.

Communication and Labeling. Specific warning information must be communicated on shipping documents, package markings and labels, placards that appear on transportation vehicles, and written emergency response information including telephone numbers to be used in case of emergencies. Properly prepared shipping documents contain, at a minimum, an identification of the hazardous material and hazard class or division number, identification number, packing group, if applicable, and total quantity shipped.

Packaging Requirements. Markings and labels should contain similar information contained on the shipping documents. Information on the packaging should easily identify that a package contains hazardous material. Any markings must be durable and readily visible. Title 49 includes specifications as to size and color of warning labels.

Operations Rules. Operating rules include processes regarding incident reporting. For example, carriers must report all incidents, which are kept in an automated Hazardous Materials Information System (HMIS) database. Any incidents involving aircraft shipments must be reported to the closest Federal Aviation Administration's Civil Aviation Security Office.

Training. All employees who perform functions in connection with hazardous materials must receive initial training and must update the training at least once every three years. If new regulations are adopted, employees must receive training on these requirements before they perform their functions again. The employer is responsible for providing the training and must keep records.

Regardless of an organization's size, several steps should be taken to manage the safe transportation of hazardous materials (Currie, 1999):

- A written compliance program, endorsed at the highest level possible, should be developed with goals and desired outcomes, organization of the agency, and training plan.
- Establish ownership and accountability throughout the organization.
- Provide systematic training to enable employees to comply with program requirements.
- Sufficient resources (money, information, personnel) will assure program success.
- There should be strict enforcement of all program provisions.
- There should be current maintenance of program and related records.

Strategy for Successful Environmental Logistics Programs

According to Gooley (1998), there are several things to consider in drawing up a step-by-step environmental plan. First, organizations need to consider why a plan is needed. There are multiple reasons, including meeting regulatory statutes, helping the environment, public opinion, and economic pressures. The EPA, for example, was authorized, under Section 6002 of the Resource Conservation and Recovery Act (RCRA) and Executive Order 13101, to designate products made with recoverable materials and recommend practices to buy these products for all federal agencies www.epa.gov/cpg. Once designated, that product must be procured with the highest practical recovered material content.

At this stage, organizations also need to consider what resources it is willing to commit or can budget to implement an environmental program. A solid waste audit will help determine the types and volumes of solid waste generated. An audit should include (a) determining what is thrown away into the dumpster; (b) a visit to the landfill; (c) interviews with employees; and (d) what waste is unique to your operation, such as vendor packaging. The budget will determine the extent of a program. If faced with limited resources, the organization may want to consider hiring a third party or transportation company.

Once the idea is accepted, how will the plan be communicated to users or internal customers? Written instructions with preprinted labels from the manufacturer, e-mails, and newsletters are some of the more common ways to ensure compliance with the program. In some cases, additional training for internal customers may need to be provided.

As an organization plans the process, it should develop a flow chart or process map, with detailed steps from origin of returns process to final disposition of waste/product. This flow chart or process map will provide a complete understanding of the internal operations and any shortcomings that could impede implementation. The map should include information about:

- *Retrieval*. Who will pick up the waste/product and how will this activity happen?

- *Special Training*. This may be required of transportation company and driver, particularly for hazardous waste.

- *Transportation*. Be sure to provide accurate information, including weight, product classification, and a description on a bill of lading.

- *Disposition*. This entails handling of returns in a centralized or regional location and how returns should be processed. Centralized locations allow for better data collection and tracking of returns to secondary markets overseas.

Develop an information system to support data collection and collect cost information. The Internet is frequently used as a part of this system. Software should facilitate the backward movement of items smoothly and efficiently. Software that captures all details of the shipment and tracks shipment status should be integrated into the system.

Finally, know the financial and credit implications of the program. There may be refunds and credits from the manufacturer and inventory cost accounting issues. Once a plan has been developed, specific goals should be set, and a plan for education and training should be developed. All measurable, time-based goals should be tracked, followed by feedback and corrective action taken when necessary.

Conclusion

Organizations have increased their efforts to be environmentally conscious and proactively pursue activities that involve reverse and green logistics activities. Many state and local agencies have implemented recycling programs to reduce pressure on landfills and improve conservation. Total cost of ownership analysis, which measures the economic and environmental effects of a product through purchase, use and disposal, is an important part of any environmental program (Kopicki, Berg, Legg, Dasappa, & Maggioni, 1993; Menezes, 2001). It is important to recognize that all supply chain members should be involved in environmental activities.

The issue of practicing environmentally effective logistics has also resulted in organizations outsourcing at least part of their reverse and green logistics functions. Third parties are increasingly meeting the needs of agencies, often customizing their services to meet specific needs. Third parties may be particularly beneficial regarding transportation and disposal of hazardous waste. As a result, third parties have begun to form strategic alliances with other logistics providers to compile a complete package of services.

References

Currie, J. V. (1999). Hazmat safety is no accident. *Logistics Management and Distribution Report, 38*(10).

Ellram, L. (1993, Fall). Total cost of ownership: Elements and implementation. *International Journal of Purchasing and Materials Management*, 2-11.

Fredette, M. (2001, April). The benefits of green purchasing. *Purchasing Today*, 54-58.

Gooley, T. B. (1998, June). Reverse logistics: Five steps to success. *Logistics Management*, 49-54.

Kopicki, R. J., Berg, M. J., Legg, L. L., Dasappa, V., & Maggioni, C. (1993). *Reuse and recycling reverse logistics opportunities*. Oak Brook, IL: Council of Logistics Management.

Menezes, S. (2001, May). Calculating the total cost of ownership. *Purchasing Today*, 16-17.

Murphy, P. R., & Poist, R. F. (2000, Winter). Green logistics strategies: An analysis of usage patterns. *Transportation Journal*, 5-16.

NE Department of Transportation, Office of the Inspector General, Research and Special Programs Administration. (2000, March). *Departmentwide program evaluation of the hazardous materials transportation programs: Executive summary*. Washington, DC: U.S. Department of Transportation.

Rogers, D., & Tibben-Lembke, R. (2001). An examination of reversal logistics practices. *Journal of Business Logistics, 22*(2), 129-148.

Schwartz, B. (2000). Reverse logistics strengthen supply chains. *Transportation and Distribution, 41*(5), 95-100.

Stock, J. R. (1998). *Development and implementation of reverse logistics programs*. Oak Brook, IL: Council of Logistics Management.

Tibben-Lembke, R. S. (1998). The impact of reverse logistics on the total cost of ownership. *Journal of Marketing Theory and Practice, 6*(4), 51-60.

United States Code Annotated. (1993). St. Paul, MN: West Publishing Company.

U.S. Environmental Protection Agency (EPA). (1999a, July). *Defending the environment at the Department of Defense*. Washington, DC: EPA:

U.S. Environmental Protection Agency (EPA). (1999b). *Municipal solid waste in the United States: 1999 final report*. Washington, DC: EPA:

Weiskott, M. N. (2000). Reverse logistics. *Supply and Distribution*. Available from www.bizsites.com.

Young, R. R. (2000, July). Supplier roles in environmental issues. *World Markets Series Business Briefing*, 59-64.

Chapter 9

Role Of Logistics In Strategic Planning

The main goal for those managing the logistics function is to provide the best possible service through a combination of customer service, transportation, warehousing, and inventory management activities. It is important that those involved know and understand the organization's overall mission, strategy, goals, and objectives in order to develop supporting strategies. This can be accomplished through the strategic planning process.

Strategic Planning

As a management tool, strategic planning is a process by which people make decisions about intended future outcomes, how outcomes are to be accomplished (i.e., strategy), and how success will be measured and evaluated. Strategic planning occurs at the highest level in an organization and should be done on a routine basis. Its purpose is to help those in an organization do their jobs better. The process may vary, but generally includes the following steps (www.griesgraber.com/planning.htm):

- Create or review the mission statement. The mission statement should address the reason for the organization's existence, its distinctive features, its core values, and who it serves.

- Develop key assumptions for development of goals and objectives, which are based on the organization's mission.

- Perform an environmental scan by gathering information about the present and expected future trends that impact the organization.

- Develop a SWOT analysis of the organization's Strengths and Weaknesses (internal factors), possible Opportunities, and Threats (external factors) to the organization's future.

- Prioritize issues raised from the environmental scan and SWOT analysis.

- Develop goals based on the issues raised.

- Invite key stakeholders to review goals before they are accepted.

- Formally adopt goals.

- Develop written objectives based on goals.

- Develop strategies, or long-term action plans, for each written objective.

Tactical Planning and Logistics

Once the strategic planning process is complete, the tactical planning process follows and should result in a plan that supports the strategic plan. Tactical planning is a lower-level process by which people make decisions about how outcomes described in the strategic plan will be accomplished, what services will be offered, how success is measured and evaluated, and how budgetary resources are allocated. Each functional area supporting the organization should do tactical planning.

Those involved in managing logistics and transportation should go through the planning process. Logistics planning has been defined as "a unified, comprehensive, and integrated planning process; anticipating future demand for logistics services; and managing the resources of the entire supply chain (and done within the overall context of the organizational plan)" (Cooper, Innis, & Dickson, 1992).

To develop a logistics plan, several steps are involved (Lambert, Stock, & Ellram, 1998). First, a logistics audit of current performance is necessary. The audit team should include anyone involved in managing or performing logistical activities. This provides the opportunity for purchasing to be an active team member. Any gaps in performance should be identified at this time. In many instances, there may be necessary trade-offs between activities that affect performance.

As part of the audit, those involved in logistics planning should perform environmental scanning, which requires looking at, and interpreting, information about trends, events, and relationships in an organization's external environment. Some major trends are affecting the way logistics activities are performed (Denali Consulting, 2003).

- Globalization of the marketplace
- eCommerce
- Reverse logistics
- eProcurement of transportation

- Integration of the supply chain
- Online track and trace capability for shipments
- Growth of third-party logistics providers (3PLs).

From this information the audit team should be able to develop a list of key issues that need further investigation. For example, the current customer service strategy may need changing, or there may be lost opportunities for cost reduction within the logistics system that need to be addressed. There also may be opportunities to outsource some or all logistics activities.

Once this list is developed, it is important to determine if logistics is meeting the organization's objectives. To assess current performance, some concrete measures will be needed. These measures should cover the effectiveness of customer service, such as order cycle times and delivery performance; the cost-efficiency of logistics, i.e., looking at the costs of inventory management, warehousing, purchasing and transportation; and determining how well assets are being utilized, including inventory, warehouses and other storage facilities, and any transportation equipment.

There... may be opportunities to outsource some or all logistics activities.

Surveying or interviewing internal and external customers is also important to determine if the current logistics system is meeting user needs and if requirements may be changing in the future. Documentation should be collected as input on current performance, including bills of lading, freight bills, order cycle times data, and fill rate data. This information can then be compiled into a standardized format, possibly in a database or spreadsheets.

Once all surveys, interviews, and data have been collected, they should be analyzed in light of the original issues raised. A proposed strategy and its expected impact on service levels can now be developed. These strategic and tactical planning activities are important processes that can lead to better organizational and logistical performance.

Tactical Planning at New Jersey-American Water Company

The New Jersey-American Water Company (NJAW) was faced with population growth that exceeded the existing capacity of its current water system (www.akleinpr.com). Residents were complaining of either no water or "dirty" water. The goals were to provide residents with a reliable source of clean water delivered through a $6 million pipeline project.

An audit was performed to assess several issues regarding installation of the new pipeline, including (a) potential traffic issues; (b) environmental issues; and (c) inconvenience to businesses, schools, and healthcare facilities. Local officials and the police department were interviewed, and they identified issues that had occurred during previous construction projects, thus providing suggestions to avoid the same problems on this project. A partnership was formed with the police department to handle traffic problems, detour routes, and other issues. Bell Atlantic (now Verizon) was also interviewed to identify any problems it encountered during its construction project in the same area.

Target audiences were invited to participate in public meetings to address concerns and answer questions regarding the project. At the meeting, attendees were asked to fill out a survey to assure that all their questions had been answered.

The team concluded that the project was viable, and an action plan was developed, including (a) development of an information kit, which was distributed to the media and local officials on the project; (b) distribution of personalized construction notices to all residents affected by the project and to the media; (c) updating of construction progress to all concerned; and (d) telephone calls to the police and others affected to address any issues during construction.

Leading Edge Logistics Management

According to a Cap Gemini Ernst & Young report (Thompson, Holcomb, & Manrodt, 2001), drivers of logistics excellence can be categorized into six components: (a) collaboration, (b) optimization, (c) connectivity, (d) execution, (e) speed, and (f) visibility.

Collaboration. Collaboration is defined in the report as the "leveraging of supply chain assets with key customers and suppliers to achieve a common goal" (Thompson et al., p. 4). Collaboration includes the sharing of real-time data with *key* suppliers and customers, alignment of individuals and organizations, and the standardization of processes and practices across organizations.

Optimization. Optimization involves using available quantitative tools to make the logistics function as efficient as possible. According to the report, organizations are moving away from manual systems and the use of spreadsheets to more sophisticated, integrated software. Some of the leading-edge tools include enterprise resource planning (ERP), transportation management systems (TMS), warehouse management systems (WMS), and order fulfillment (Bowersox, Closs, & Cooper, 2002). An ERP system is software that replaces an organization's "legacy" applications by providing integrated modules and one database. (Legacy applications were developed before 1990 to individually perform various operations, including ordering and inventory management.) ERP systems can make logistics and supply chain operations easier through order entry, order fulfillment, and procurement capabilities. ERP systems also include financial, accounting, and human resource modules. WMS and TMS are additional software packages that can be integrated into an existing ERP system to facilitate exchange of data among all areas of the organization. TMS usually contain routing, consolidation, management of reverse logistics, and load building functions. WMS help improve warehouse management through receiving, storage, shipping, and warehouse automation functions.

Connectivity. Connectivity describes the level of integration among individuals and organizations in information-sharing. High levels of integration mean that a greater standardization of software applications and platforms is in place, which improves collaboration and allows for trade exchanges. Connectivity also means that less uncertainty exists in the supply chain and lower inventory levels.

Execution. The ability to improve all areas of logistics, including transportation, inventory management, warehousing, and order fulfillment, are aspects of execution. Organizations also have the capability to measure performance results and then use those results to improve the operation even further.

Speed. Speed involves the ability to improve responsiveness and be adaptive to changing situations. Speed is possible because real-time data is available.

Visibility is the ability to make the logistics system "transparent." Inventory can be tracked; the status of an order is readily available; and incidents can be managed online.

Visibility. Visibility is the ability to make the logistics system "transparent." Inventory can be tracked; the status of an order is readily available; and incidents can be managed online. A follow-up Cap Gemini Ernst & Young study (Montgomery, Holcomb, & Manrodt, 2002) suggests that visibility is the most critical driver of change in the supply chain. Purchasing was also found to be the most frequent user of logistics information, including order status, tracking of inbound shipments, and notification of delayed shipments.

There are some inherent risks in these drivers that should be mentioned. Many organizations, for example, have become dependent on real-time connectivity and run into problems when systems are not functioning. Manual back-up systems are still required. There is also a certain level of exposure as organizations become more strategically integrated and share information to a greater extent. Carefully written contracts and routine performance measurement of suppliers are important when addressing security issues. Transparency requires significant initial investments in technology as well as continuous investments as software is updated. Overall, inherent in these drivers is a significant adjustment to change, which has its own challenges. Some managers may not see the current processes as "broken" and, therefore, see no reason to "fix them." As Michael Hammer stated, "The technical problems—dealing with Internet architecture, data sharing, synchronization, and so on—are easy. The hard problems are getting people to change their behavior." That's true of any major initiative (Anonymous, 2001/2002).

Changes in logistical processes must also be seen as long term, requiring careful planning and leadership. New technologies and processes should be adopted as a part of an overall integrative plan. A cost/benefit analysis should be a part of any recommended changes to the current process.

However, multiple success stories can be found in industry. Pier 1 Imports has addressed several drivers of logistics and supply chain excellence, including visibility, optimization, speed, and connectivity (www.manufacturing.net/lm/index).

Pier 1 Imports

Pier 1 Imports was experiencing problems with inventory visibility in its six distribution centers located in the United States. Because paper forms were used to transfer information between its central computer in Fort Worth, Texas, and the distribution centers, inventory was often moved before the Distribution Center's information systems were updated. As a result, Pier 1 was having trouble determining the exact location of warehouse stock, incoming inventory, or outgoing shipments.

The company purchased software that allowed it to track any inbound inventory from the time a shipment left the supplier's site to the moment it reached one of Pier 1's distribution centers. The supplier provides information on each stock-keeping unit (SKU) as well as from each transportation provider. Details of incoming shipments and expected arrival times are now available in real-time. This information is particularly important when Pier 1 purchases goods based on an F.O.B. origin basis because Pier 1 now knows what inventory each supplier holds.

Conclusion

About 40 years ago, logistics was recognized as an area of significance in the procurement cycle. Since then, much has been learned, and the field of logistics is an exciting one today. Multiple opportunities are available to improve logistics performance. Whether directly or indirectly involved in logistics activities, the reader has hopefully gained an appreciation of the field and realizes its importance to procurement. Greater involvement in transportation and logistics decisions can lead to improved service and increased savings to procurement's "customers," whether internal or external.

References

Anonymous (2001/2002, December/January). (Re)Made in the U.S.A. *Context Online.* Available from www.con-text.com.

Bowersox, D. J., Closs, D. J., & Cooper, M. B. (2002). *Supply chain logistics management.* Boston: McGraw Hill.

Cooper, M. C., Innis, D. E., & Dickson, P. R. (1992). *Strategic planning for logistics.* Oak Brook, IL: Council of Logistics Management.

Denali Consulting. (2003). *Logistics trends—Achieving supply chain integration.* San Francisco: Denali Consulting.

Lambert, D. M., Stock, J. R., & Ellram, L. M. (1998). *Fundamentals of logistics management.* Boston: Irwin McGraw-Hill.

Montgomery, A., Holcomb, M. C., & Manrodt, K. B. (2002). *Visibility: Tactical solutions, strategic implications.* Chicago, IL: Cap Gemini Ernst & Young.

Thompson, R. H., Holcomb, M. C., & Manrodt, K. B. (2001). *Transforming logistics: A roadmap to logistics excellence.* Chicago, IL: Cap Gemini Ernst & Young.

Index

About the Authors

L inda L. Stanley is an adjunct professor for Arizona State University, teaching supplier management and negotiations. Previously she was a visiting professor at Arizona State University West and associate professor and chair of the Management Department at Our Lady of the Lake University, in San Antonio, Texas. She earned a BA at California State University, a BS in Accounting and a Ph.D. in Business Administration from Arizona State University. Prior to her academic career, Dr. Stanley worked in the mortgage banking and savings and loan industries. Her research interests include internal service quality, purchasing performance, and the buyer/supplier relationship. She has published articles in several journals, including *Journal of Operations Management*, *Journal of Supply Chain Management*, and *Journal of Business Logistics*. Dr. Stanley has coauthored two other books, *Process Management: Creating Value along the Supply Chain*, released in 2007, and *Effective Supply Management Performance*, due out in 2007.

D arin Matthews currently serves as chief procurement officer for Metro regional government in Portland, Oregon. He has nearly 20 years of purchasing and supply management experience in state and local government, as well as private industry. He is a past-president of the Oregon Public Purchasing Association and a former board member of NAPM - Willamette Valley. Darin speaks throughout the US and Canada on a variety of procurement topics, and his writings have been featured in *Purchasing Today*, *Government Procurement*, *The Public Manager* and *The Journal of Public Procurement*. The co-author of two supply management texts through Florida Atlantic University and NIGP, he has also been published by the Australian Institute of Purchasing and Materials Management. Darin is a Certified Public Purchasing Officer (CPPO) and a Certified Purchasing Manager (C.P.M.). He holds a Bachelor's degree in Business/Political Science and a Master's Certificate in Acquisition Management. Darin is a Master Instructor for the National Institute of Governmental Purchasing and has served on their Board of Directors since 2001.

Other books published by
NIGP: The Institute for Public Procurement:

INTRODUCTION TO PUBLIC PROCUREMENT

CONTRACT ADMINISTRATION

THE LEGAL ASPECTS OF PUBLIC PROCUREMENT

DEVELOPING AND MANAGING REQUESTS FOR PROPOSALS IN THE PUBLIC SECTOR

STRATEGIC PROCUREMENT PLANNING IN THE PUBLIC SECTOR

SOURCING IN THE PUBLIC SECTOR

FUNDAMENTALS OF LEADERSHIP AND MANAGEMENT IN PUBLIC PROCUREMENT

ALTERNATIVE DISPUTE RESOLUTION

CONTRACTING FOR PUBLIC SECTOR SERVICES

CAPITAL ACQUISITIONS

RISK MANAGEMENT IN PUBLIC CONTRACTING

WAREHOUSE AND INVENTORY CONTROL

CONTRACTING FOR CONSTRUCTION SERVICES

NOTES:

NOTES: